*To Mary, with lo*

# AUTHOR *Mitchell L. Hewson, HTR, HTM, LT RHCP*

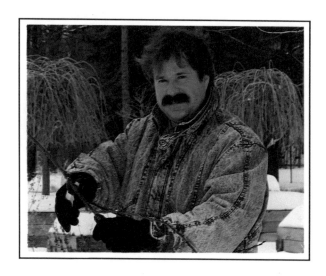

**H**umanist, naturalist, horticultural therapist, Mitchell Hewson, HTM is the heart and driving force behind horticultural therapy in Canada.

Mitchell Hewson was the first Registered Horticultural Therapist to practice in Canada. He was a chartered member of the Canadian Horticultural Therapy Association and a past Board Member of the American Horticultural Therapy Association. He lectures and conducts workshops internationally and is a popular radio and television guest. Mitchell's articles have appeared in many Canadian and American magazines and newspapers. His book *Horticulture as Therapy* was presented the American Horticultural Therapy Publication Award and has been translated into Japanese. Mitchell received the Alice Burlingame Humanitarian Service Award for promoting and furthering horticultural therapy.

Mitchell Hewson is the professional discipline leader of Horticultural Therapy at the Homewood Health Centre. His horticultural therapy program, the largest in Canada, has attracted internship students from Canada, the United States and Japan.

# Table of Contents

# Foreword

We are facing challenges and opportunities in the delivery of mental health services. In order to provide a comprehensive approach to care and meet our patients' needs, a spectrum of assessment and treatment modalities should be available.

Our clinical experience at Homewood Health Centre has shown successful therapeutic interventions using horticulture therapy. This therapy can complement other approaches or, occasionally, it could be the tool to help individuals begin to engage in a therapeutic journey.

At Homewood, we have benefitted from Mitchell Hewson's excellent horticultural therapist skills. He has had many years of experience working with diverse client groups. His expertise is highly regarded by the consumers, including other members of the interdisciplinary team.

In this book, Mitchell shares with us his insightful approach to horticulture therapy, using a client-centered focus. His book is comprehensive. It provides a sound theoretical and practical approach to different care settings.

Mitchell has made an excellent contribution to the mental health field. This book will help us to develop a better understanding of horticultural therapy and its significant contribution in the healing process. ❧

Edgardo L. Pérez, MD, MPH, FRCP(C), DABPN, CHE
Executive Vice President and Chief of Staff
Homewood Health Centre
Guelph, Ontario, Canada

Professor
Department of Psychiatry
University of Toronto
Toronto, Ontario, Canada

# Acknowledgements

Writing this book has been a long-standing dream of mine. That it has now been realized is due in no small measure to those who gave so generously of their help and support.

I would like to thank the Homewood Health Centre and, in particular, Dr. Ronald Pond, Executive Director, whose initial efforts launched this project; Dr. Edgardo Pérez, Executive Vice President and Chief of Staff, for his enthusiastic encouragement; Homewood library and archives for permission to use photographic material; Steven Davis, Executive Director, American Horticultural Therapy Association, for his invaluable and thorough editorial input; Patsy Marshall, who read the manuscript and added her critical comments; Jack Van Klavern, who generously donated photographic material and clip art; John Camelford, whose photography documents a large part of this book; Marti Sharpe, who also supplied photographs; Eleanor Hornsby, for the use of her graceful calligraphy; and finally, Frank Vadori, who did the drawings for the raised bed design and the pot-lifter.

Mitchell Hewson

# Introduction

In Canada there are very few horticultural therapists. Horticultural therapy is usually carried out by other health care professionals who facilitate a variety of programs, including horticulture as an activity or adjunctive therapy. Each discipline brings its own expertise and perspective to this therapy.

This book has been written in order to share my twenty years of experience as a horticultural therapist, working in a psychiatric hospital, using horticulture as a therapeutic tool. *Horticulture As Therapy* is intended to serve as a guide to the practice of using this form of therapy, rather than as an authority on horticulture. The purpose of this publication is to help start a therapeutic program and to keep it alive and growing.

Here at Homewood Health Centre, we are fortunate enough not only to have a greenhouse, but 47 acres of garden and bush. As you will see, our program is largely self-sustaining since we grow much of what we use. If you are utilizing a solarium or using windows, you will experience some of the same mobility. Many plants can be grown in containers on a deck or similar space. Local conservation areas can provide hiking trails for nature walks with knowledgeable staff. Grow lights in the fall and winter months can greatly enhance your program. However you set your program in motion, it will be well worth your while.

I have seen before my eyes, the spiritual growth clients undergo. Discovering the wonders of nature can represent a profound change of lifestyle for drug addicts who are learning to feel positive about themselves once more. By nurturing plants and developing an awareness of the environment, they are then able to give back these newly found skills and renewed energy to their families as well as to the community they once rejected. For people who are elderly, there is a rekindling of the desire to live and to do something meaningful. Gardening provides the schizophrenic population with a chance to hold onto reality and to master their environment. The depressed client's mood is altered in the greenhouse setting.

Negative emotions are channelled through a constructive activity which promotes optimism, confidence and self-worth.

Clients are assisted in attaining positive social and work skills by volunteers who give of their time and talent. These skills can then help build self esteem and enrich lives. Channelling negative and creative energy into horticulture not only relieves anxiety, but fosters growth and imagination.

There is something magical and curative about the powers of nature as seen in the growth of a plant. Flowers perpetuate themselves with their seeds, constantly repeating the cycle. Nature is forgiving—if a plant dies, another can be grown in its place. If a mistake is made, nature teaches how to avoid repeating it, because the life cycle of plants provides us with hope of life renewed and a chance to begin again.

Personnel working in the following types of institutions will find this book a useful resource:
- Educational institutions—horticultural and health science departments
- Hospitals—public and psychiatric
- Long term care facilities
- Vocational schools
- Residential settings for special populations
- Rehabilitation centres
- Correctional centres
- Community and social agencies
- Horticulture and landscape industry.

CHAPTER

*1*

# *What is Horticultural Therapy?*

"**H**orticultural therapy is the use of plants and gardening activities as vehicles in professionally conducted programs in therapy and rehabilitation." (Steven Davis, President, American Horticultural Therapy Association).

Another way to respond to this is to explain the dynamics of how a horticultural therapist works with clients. When clients are admitted to the Homewood Health Centre, I meet with the inter-disciplinary treatment team which consists of the following health care personnel—psychiatrist or general practitioner, social worker, nurse, occupational and recreation therapist, psychologist and program assistant. After discussing the history of events and precipitating problems leading up to admission and after standard physical and mental assessments are administered, the client and the treatment team collaborate on a plan of action. Programs and therapeutic sessions are established to comprise the client's treatment plan.

What makes horticultural therapy unique is that it uses living material, requiring nurturing and care, in its programs. The maturation and lifecycle of plants provide plenty of horticultural tasks and related activities to stimulate thought, exercise the body and encourage an awareness of the living, external environment.

Clients are encouraged to attend these programs to work through individual treatment goals. Before the process begins, we discuss their involvement to make sure they understand the relationship between horticultural therapy and their personal treatment. This ensures consistent quality of care. Clients are then divided into special groups to promote or maintain the highest functioning level. Clients who attend a program voluntarily show an interest and commitment in getting involved in treatment.

Classes, assessments or individual treatment for clients are all done in the greenhouse, plant areas and outdoor garden. (See *Year Round-Calendar of Activities*).

In carrying out the treatment plan, the horticultural therapist maintains the dual role of therapist and horticulturalist. Obviously, the client comes first and the plants and projects are secondary.

A subtle approach allows you to get to know the person more easily. Allowing yourself time to get to know someone brings greater rewards in building a trusting relationship. A therapeutic relationship and rapport can be built by working through individual or group projects. This rapport can be built by demonstrating sincerity and a sense of caring. When you encourage honest and open communication, clients are able to share their feelings and concerns.

> *A therapeutic relationship and rapport can be built by working through individual or group projects. This rapport can be built by demonstrating sincerity and a sense of caring.* ❧

Be aware of subtle changes in mood, appearance and attitude. Also be aware of special events in the client's life which could explain mood or behaviour. Know what medication the client is using because some chemicals cause side effects as well as a reaction to the sun, e.g., neuroleptics. (See *Medication*).

In a group session always seek out the quiet and nonresponsive client, since they need to feel part of the group as well. Listen intently and be sincere. Do not assume that clients like to be called by first names; ask them how they would like to be addressed. Share important events in your life with clients who are elderly. Appropriate touch is very important; a gentle hand or a kind gesture show that you care. Always give praise or reinforcement when a job has been successfully completed. Provide short-term projects for clients who will benefit from instant gratification.

Notice what your clients wear and be complimentary. Provide aprons for protection from soil and other materials.

Client success is your success; be open for change. A client may offer an alternative method of plant care, e.g., the use of soap and water or alcohol to treat an infested plant instead of spraying with a chemical.

Client interaction and activity should always be documented. These observations and written reports are then communicated to the team to assist in the evaluation of the client's progress and ongoing treatment.

## Criteria that May Jeopardize Your Program

Never allow your own personal judgement or biases to interfere when working with clients. Be careful not to allow the client to get locked into a train of thought such as "I can't do this," as this does not allow for change or progress. Do not combine clients who have different physical and mental problems, since this can also hinder progress. Do not allow clients to get bored or disinterested with material presented, keep delivery and content exciting and current! Always provide projects and tasks that are a challenge and that will meet clients' levels of functioning. Projects should be interesting and meaningful and not just busy work. Change your activities or project to parallel a seasonal event.

Have a set time for programs and do not allow a drop-in centre approach. When clients come and go as they wish without structure or commitment, this prevents continuity. Be organized; have all materials and plants ready for work sessions. Do not put expectations onto clients who are already stressed and cannot handle pressure.

Complicated tasks and poor instruction add to a sense of confusion and failure. Ask the client what he or she enjoys doing in horticulture. Know the client's likes or dislikes; read his or her chart (if access is allowed), so that you know the history of the individual. Never make decisions for clients, but allow them to come to a guided conclusion. Be careful of counter transference; do not get caught up with a client's emotions. Generally speaking, when a client says "I can't do it," this signals a sense of fear and frustration in trying. Gentle persuasion and guided demonstration are needed to turn these negative feelings into the positive response, "I'll try!"

## Dynamics of a Successful Horticultural Program

1. A good rapport with hospital staff is essential to ensure clients are dressed, fed and medicated before the program begins.
2. Always use non-poisonous plants and plants that are easily grown. (See *Useful Plants for Starting a Horticultural Therapy Program*).
3. Confidentiality is imperative in all client interaction.
4. Enrich your program with volunteer support. Volunteers are a great source of help in many areas.
5. Maintain a record or calendar of events to determine the most successful activities and plants used in your program.
6. Field trips provide stimulation for the clients, staff and volunteers. Botanical gardens, parks, and horticultural shows are just some the sites you can visit.
7. Films and guest lecturers add dimension to your program, providing stimulation and a break from regular activities.
8. If there is a problem obtaining money for needed supplies, contact businesses that supply these horticultural items and ask for a donation or a reduced price.
9. Contact local florists or funeral homes for donations of flowers. Send a card of thanks to the florist or family so that they know their efforts are appreciated.
10. The key to a successful program is to relax, be yourself, and enjoy your clients. (See *Year-Round Calendar of Activities*).

## The Role of the Horticultural Therapist in the Interdisciplinary Team

Each member of the team works towards the same goals and objectives with the client, but from the approach and perspective of their own discipline. This allows the therapist to use his or her particular skills to focus on the client's needs. Through horticultural tasks, the horticultural therapist can assess, promote and analyze the client's physical functioning, cognition and perception, emotional status and social skills.

### Physical Functioning

Through a variety of tasks and projects, the physical functioning of the client can be restored, improved, maintained or helped, to prevent further deterioration. Raised beds and patio areas can be adapted for clients with special needs. Gardening can provide needed exercise, building endurance, coordination and strength. Horticultural tasks can be adapted to develop motor skills and fine, eye-hand coordination. Plants provide a variety of physical shapes, sizes, scents and textures to help clients decipher the environment.

### Cognition and Perception

Horticulture plays a major role in determining the clients' level of functional ability through a variety of tasks. (See *Projects for the Cognitively Impaired*). Clients are evaluated on their ability to understand and comprehend. Simple or complex procedural testing, concentration, retention and method interpretation can be scored.

Using the medium of plants, horticulture provides excellent stimuli through vision, smell, taste, touch and texture, via the perception and recognition of plants. The greenhouse and garden environment can set the tone for comprehension and realization; that is, the structure of the greenhouse is associated with the growing of plants and the garden with growing vegetables and flowers.

### Reality Awareness

Horticultural projects can provide an awareness of time and seasonal events. Problem solving techniques and skills can be learned.

### Educational Experience

Learning about horticulture can stimulate the client into other areas of horticulture.

### Emotional Status

The horticultural area sets the tone for a positive and nonthreatening environment. Through individual or group interaction, clients are encouraged to understand and to deal with their emotions and feelings. Horticultural projects and activities build clients' skill levels, self esteem and confidence. Tasks such as pruning, smashing pots and hoeing provide an acceptable outlet for anger and aggression. Classes in design and flower arranging provide an outlet for creativity and imagination.

Working with plants fosters a sense of nurturing. Horticultural tasks and projects also provide structure and activity to help elevate depression and alter negative feelings.

When working with clients who are elderly, there is at times a concern as to whether the client has a form of dementia or underlying depression. Horticultural tasks and assessment can help determine which diagnosis is appropriate.

### Social Skills

The horticultural therapy program is an excellent area to develop and build good interaction with clients. Working on a project allows the therapist to build a rapport with the client without direct confrontation. Through the therapeutic dynamics in the program, the therapist is able to rate the client's social functioning level by observing if the client 1) tends to isolate himself or herself; 2) works independently; 3) tends to exhibit socially appropriate behaviour and 4) works with other group members. Working in a group setting provides interaction through sharing materials and tools to complete a project.

## *Horticultural Therapy Assessment*

Once treatment goals have been set by the interdisciplinary team, the horticultural therapist can use horticultural tasks or activities as tools to assess the client's abilities and skill levels. It is important to note however that these assessments can only be done by a professional horticultural therapist.

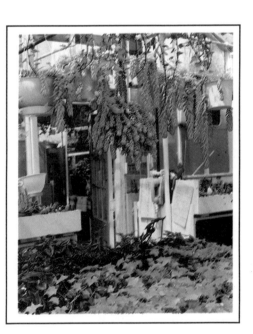

The greenhouse or solarium provides a pleasant, natural and non-threatening environment where the client's reactions to horticulture as a therapeutic medium can be gauged. The therapist assesses functioning levels from a physical and psychological perspective. Continued assessment of the client's involvement evaluates responses to goals and objectives of the treatment team. The therapist should share assessment results with clients who are not cognitively impaired and can understand the significance of their responses to the following categories. (See **TABLE 1, HORTI-CULTURAL THERAPY ASSESSMENT**).

### Cognitive Skills
These refer to the process of comprehension, judgment, memory and reason.

### Physical Skills
This is based on the client's ability to perform specific motor skills through a given task.

### Behavioural and Social Skills
Clients are assessed as to their attitude, manner and ability to relate to others.

### The Assessment Area
Clients with cognitive and/or physical problems must be assisted by staff or volunteers to the program area.

The work area should be organized and ready to begin. Arrange the seating so that you are close to the client to better interact and provide support. Always introduce yourself and other staff and volunteers. Wear a name tag.

Based on the client's history and your observations, determine a time frame to be spent in the assessment area that does not exceed the client's comfort levels. Speak clearly and give instructions so that they are easily understood. Always make the clients feel comfortable and allow them to express their feelings, giving praise when it is appropriate.

> *Always make the clients feel comfortable and allow them to express their feelings, giving praise when it's appropriate.* ❧

Begin with a project such as transplanting. This provides a physical activity that can be used as a testing device for scoring a client's abilities and basic understanding. For best results, divide the task into a number of sequences so you can determine how many step procedures the client can achieve. Use the common names of plants and demonstrate with a hands-on technique. Once you have demonstrated the method, allow clients to repeat the process on their own. Repeat this procedure until you have learned what stages can be handled unassisted. If this task is beyond the client's capabilities, determine what step procedures they can do with assistance. This assessment will provide the following data:

**Cognitive Skills**

1. Is the client oriented to time and place? This helps to determine the client's mental functioning status: disorientation, lack of awareness or confusion.
2. Does the client know what season of the year it is? This helps you evaluate how familiar and conscious of the environment the client is.
3. Does the client remember your name? This determines the client's immediate memory, especially for those who may have a possible memory loss or form of dementia.
4. Does the client remember the name of the plant? This indicates the client's short-term memory and may stimulate past memories and old work skills.
5. Can the client identify tools and horticultural mediums? This assists you in discovering the client's ability to perceive, represent and organize objects in relationships appropriate to the task at hand, i.e., transplanting, using soil, plants and plant medium.
6. Does the client understand the performance standards? This will indicate the client's ability to perceive quality and quantity of work completed.
7. How long is the client's attention span? This time period indicates the time the client was able to concentrate on the task.
8. Can the client complete the task accurately, and if not, how many steps was he or she able to complete? If the task is completed accurately, this establishes the level of intellectual and perceptual accomplishment. When the client is unable to complete a sequential step procedure, this may indicate deficiencies in other areas of the client's functioning levels, i.e., memory and cognitive functioning.
9. Does this activity stimulate old work skills? Skills are easily relearned when they are based on memories of past work experiences.

**Physical Skills**

1. Are there any physical problems that interfere with the client's ability to do this task? The physical assessment is an excellent indicator in determining strengths and deficits in the client's physical functioning. Observe motor skill functions such as the execution of tasks bilaterally, or by left or right hand. Determine if the client is able to hold onto tools and objects.

2. What are the physical problems? List any concerns. Identify the client's physical impairment such as contractures, arthritis, paralysis or degenerative diseases. Would these clients benefit from physical medicine or physical skills to improve or prevent further deterioration or retard dysfunctional processes?

3. Can tools or the physical environment be adapted to increase the client's ability to do this task? Tools and environment can be adapted to meet the client's capabilities. (See *Adapting Special Tools*).

4. Does the client have good eyesight? Tasks such as transplanting require the client to spoon soil from one area to another; this task requires good eyesight. A pattern of miscalculating distance and spooning-up uneven amounts of soil can indicate problems with eyesight and the need for further investigation and corrective treatment.

5. Does the client have good eye-hand coordination? This determines the client's ability to perceive space and execute fine motor movements.

6. Does the client hear properly? It is important to recognize the client's auditory responses. Be aware of the ability to hear stimuli and respond accordingly. Determine the degree of the deficit, e.g., hears high pitch noises, or only hears from one side.

7. Does the client experience pain during the activity? Be acquainted with any pain or physical complaints. Remember to keep within the client's limitations to prevent further deterioration or injury. Pain can alter the client's responses to a task, limiting his or her involvement in the horticultural activity.

8. Does the client have enough energy to complete the task? The work output indicates the client's stamina and potential strength. The task can be extended or limited to suit the client's needs.

9. Will this task improve physical function? Determine the client's capabilities, then improve or modify the task to build strength, maintain function and prevent further physical deterioration.

10. Does medication affect the client's physical abilities? Be aware of medication that may cause side effects and alter the client's abilities to complete the task from a physical viewpoint.

**Behaviour Skills**

1. What is the client's attitude towards this activity? The client's conduct and perception of this activity will define how effectively the client performs the task.

2. What is the client's mood and how does this affect the activity? The client's emotional behaviour sets the tone for his or her insight, judgment and accomplishments. Ongoing assessment in this area may result in the restructuring of the activity to elevate or alter behaviour.

3. Does the client display appropriate behaviour? The interaction and conduct of the client working on a project indicates the suitability of his or her performance (social behaviour).

4. Is the client able to articulate concerns and feelings? It is essential for the therapist and client to build a therapeutic rapport to assist the client in expressing emotions and problems.

5. Does the client demonstrate good hygiene? This determines the client's understanding of what is socially acceptable when working with others.

6. Is the client able to express emotions and thoughts about the plants around them? This determines the client's depth of involvement and insights about the therapeutic medium, i.e., value of plants.

7. Has there been any change in the client's behaviour?  During the course of treatment has the client exhibited any change in conduct or performance?

## Social Skills

1. Is there a language or cultural barrier?  To be able to communicate effectively with the client there must be an understanding of the client's language and culture.  If there is a problem, volunteers or staff who can speak the language are sometimes brought in to assist.
2. Is there a physical barrier, such as, a hearing or medical problem?  Find out through your assessment if there is a hearing loss or medical problem that can inhibit understanding.

## Summation

This evaluation can be done with a variety of horticultural tasks.  Through the above assessment, the therapist can change or alter the treatment plan to best meet the needs of the client. There should be ongoing documentation of the client's response to treatment in the horticultural therapy program in the form of progress notes.

# TABLE 1

## HORTICULTURAL THERAPY ASSESSMENT

CLIENT NAME: ...........................................................................................................

DOCTOR:....................................................................................................................

UNIT OR WARD: .......................................................................................................

GOALS: ......................................................................................................................

...................................................................................................................................

...................................................................................................................................

THERAPIST: ..............................................................................................................

DATE: .......................................................

**COGNITIVE SKILLS:**

1.  Is the client oriented to time and place?

2.  Does the client know the time of season?

3.  Does the client remember your name?

4.  Does the client remember the name of the plant?

5.  Can the client identify the tools and horticultural mediums?

6.  Does the client understand the performance standards?

7.  How long is the client's attention span?

8.  Can the client complete the task accurately? If not, how many steps can he/she complete?

9.  Can the client learn new work skills?

10. Does this activity stimulate old work skills?

## PHYSICAL SKILLS

1. Are there any physical problems that interfere with the client's ability to do this task?

2. What are the physical problems? List any concerns.

3. Can tools or the physical environment be adapted to increase the client's ability to do this task?

4. Does the client have good eyesight?

5. Does the client have good eye-hand coordination?

6. Does the client hear properly?

7. Does the client experience pain during the activity?

8. Does the client have enough energy to complete the task?

9. Will this task improve physical function?

10. Does medication affect the client's physical abilities?

## BEHAVIOURAL SKILLS

1. What is the client's attitude regarding this activity?

2. What is the client's mood and effect toward this activity?

3. Does the client demonstrate socially appropriate behaviour?

4. Is the client able to express concerns and feelings?

5. Does the client demonstrate good hygiene?

6. Is the client able to express emotions or thoughts about the plants around her or him?

7. Has there been any change in the client's behaviour?

## SOCIAL SKILLS

1. Is there a language or cultural barrier?

2. Is there a physical barrier, e.g., hearing or medical problem?

*Please note: The above assessment can be used to develop outcome indicators for quality management.*

## Therapeutic Dynamics

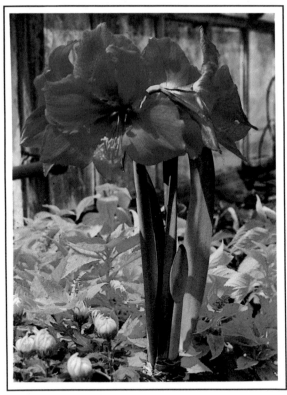

*Amaryllis*

A horticultural therapist utilizes plants and plant-related activities as a therapeutic medium to enhance physical, emotional, social and spiritual well-being. The following examples of clients' experiences in horticultural therapy will illustrate this definition.

🌺 An elderly woman who had been depressed for a long period of time habitually isolated herself. Given an amaryllis bulb for Christmas, she planted it with little enthusiasm, and kept it in her bathroom where she watered it occasionally. Soon after, she was surprised to see something emerge. The stem began to sprout at a rapid rate, which so thrilled her she felt it should be moved to her bedroom for her roommate to see. This amazing growth continued, and she was delighted when the first bloom appeared. Now, she wanted to share it with others and moved it to the main lounge area where everyone could view the spectacular beauty of the plant that she had grown herself. This formerly reclusive woman was now talking, sharing and socializing with others because of this positive experience.

In order for a plant to survive, it needs care, water, sunlight and fertilizer. Working with a small responsibility, this client came to experience her own worth and the value of her existence.

🌺 A former model who had undergone a recent mastectomy was admitted with the diagnosis of major depression, with suicidal ideation. Symptoms included poor eating and sleeping patterns, and little interest in activity or life itself. She also experienced periods of crying and despair.

The client was referred to the horticultural therapy program, where she went through the motions of planting and caring for plants. This obviously did not meet her needs, as she became more depressed and withdrawn. She was introduced next to the Floral Design Program, where she was exposed to colour, beauty and design. Within a short period of time her skill level was excellent and she seemed to take great pride in the design pieces she created. This woman appeared more confident and her attitude towards life was more optimistic. She was less weepy and her energy and activity levels increased. Before she was discharged, she visited local florists and spoke with other designers to get a feeling for the business. She has since opened up her own florist store and is doing very well. This client realized that although she might have lost some of her beauty, she was now able to create beauty that was an extension of herself. Physical beauty may fade or lessen, but inner beauty and worth are fostered and promoted through creativity and imagination.

❧ A man in his early forties was admitted with a diagnosis of alcohol dependency. Because of his alcohol abuse he had patterns of instability in his job and family relationships. When working in the greenhouse, he was surprised to see the effects of over-watered plants, especially a large jade plant. The plant was becoming very yellow and sickly. He made the connection, realizing the same thing was happening to him because of his disease process. It was this symbiotic relationship that helped him to acknowledge his alcohol addiction. The client went on to acquire good skills in horticulture, particularly in landscaping. Since discharge, he has changed his life style, using his leisure time for gardening and neighbourhood landscaping. Follow-up has shown that he now has a stable work pattern and stronger bonds with his family.

❧ A young mother, aged 27, who had been diagnosed with cancer and given approximately six months to live, was admitted with feelings of despair and hopelessness. When her family came to visit she tended to close herself off from them. The psychiatrist was hoping to stabilize her with medication, to assist her in developing coping mechanisms for her limited future. This woman was so despondent that she would not leave her room, or get involved with any treatment programs. The doctor in charge admitted he could not motivate her to get involved with any possible psychological treatment. The client's family was also suffering and they spoke to the doctor about how difficult they found it to visit, as she would not respond to her husband or three children.

I was asked to get her involved with some programs. When I went to visit her, I took three roses from a bouquet she had been given and said "these roses are dying, but they are still capable of delivering life and beauty just as you could share your life and beauty with your family during the time you have left." This statement seemed to awaken something in the client and she became very angry and wept. She spoke of her inability to deal with her imminent death and her denial of it and mourned the short time left for her to live. This led to other sessions where the client was able to talk and begin to deal with how the remainder of her time should be spent. This client soon became actively involved in programs, such as making terrariums and floral design pieces for others. She also was able to deal more constructively and openly with family members. This led to her discharge in a much shorter period of time.

❧ An elderly man was admitted with a diagnosis of reactive depression brought on by the death of his wife. He had once been a very active man who liked to be busy. Unfortunately, the death of his wife had left him depressed, with little interest in life and weak from inactivity and lack of exercise. He was referred to the horticultural therapy program. With encouragement, he was able to do a range of activities from propagating plants to planting vegetables in containers and raised beds. I learned that this client had been a farmer for many years before he retired. He was happy to share his experience and skills with others. He has since left the hospital and built raised containers and planters on his balcony. This activity gave him another chance to use his old work skills to provide beauty and something to care for beyond himself.

In the above scenarios, horticulture played a significant role in turning these lives around.

- The first client realized that the plant did respond to care; more importantly, she herself responded to the care and nurturing that was given her, thereby developing a sense of self worth and responsibility, which allowed her to share this positive experience with others.

- The second client responded to horticultural therapy in a different way. Initially, the client was merely going through the motions of work, and did not benefit from this activity. Realizing this, the therapist was able to alter the activity to include more creative tasks to meet her need for narcissistic gratification. This client was not losing her beauty, but through her creative skills, and with a change of attitude, discovered the inner beauty of self worth and acceptance.

- The man who was an alcoholic needed to discover for himself that he was an alcoholic. The turning point in this man's life came as a result of the plants he was caring for, deteriorating from over watering. This analogy helped him to understand the cause and effect of his substance abuse. The result was the development of a leisure skill and the self-worth derived from this pastime.

- The young mother diagnosed with cancer came to terms with her illness. The turning point was not working with plants, but rather the plant acting as a catalyst with which she could sublimate her pain and anger.

- The elderly gentleman was diagnosed with reactive depression as a result of the many losses in his life. These events led him to a state of despair and hopelessness. The program provided him with the opportunity to discover his strengths and abilities. He was able to reconnect with old work skills, which altered the degree of his loss and gave him a sense of purpose and hope.

# Starting a Horticultural Therapy Program

W hen starting a horticultural therapy program, the first step is to contact management for permission to speak to clients and staff. This will let you evaluate the need for a horticultural therapy program. Explain to both clients and staff the therapeutic benefits of this type of therapy and find out what they would like to accomplish with such a program.

**Location**
Find an area where you would like to do this program, remembering that the location must be accessible for wheelchairs and the physically challenged. At the Homewood we have a wheelchair lift and ramps.

For an indoor program, natural light is crucial to the success of growing plants. Most institutions and hospitals do not have the luxury of a greenhouse or solarium, but there are excellent areas that can be developed for growing plants inside. Rooms that have large windows facing either east or south provide good light for most plants. Tables can be adapted or put in front of these windows, with trays to catch excess water. Grow lights are great for areas that have no access to sufficient light. These lights can be three-tiered stands or units that fit over a bed or wheelchair. (See **Resources**).

Wherever your location is, it is important to provide humidity for your plants by misting them or setting them in a tray with pebbles so that the plants are not soaking up the water. The pebbles allow the moisture to be diffused around the plant. Provide good air circulation by opening windows in the summer and have a fan going at all times.

Outside areas can be located anywhere, as long as there is at least a half day of sunshine. Shade is essential for clients who cannot tolerate the sun. Raised beds are suitable for those who like to garden from a standing or sitting position. These beds are easily adapted to hospital areas where they provide a pocket of colour or a quiet space for those who appreciate nature. (See *Resources* and *Raised Bed Gardening*).

## Staffing

Contact horticultural societies, master gardeners, botanical gardens, civic garden centres, volunteer agencies, etc. If you can network with Occupation and Recreation departments in your area, they can assist you with many of the medical and physical needs of clients.

## Budget

Determine your budget needs, determine the cost of supplies by the number of clients and activities you wish to do.

## Population

Determine the population you are going to work with.

## Goals

Determine what your goals and objectives are in this program and how they relate to the overall mission statement or philosophy of the institution. Develop a format under the following headings:

1. **Name** of the horticultural therapy group, e.g., Gardening for Health and Leisure.

2. **Purpose**, e.g., the horticultural therapy program utilizes plants and plant-related mediums to enhance or rehabilitate the physical, social and emotional well-being of people.

3. **Goals and Objectives**
   - To provide clients with an opportunity to build self-esteem through a meaningful activity with living material.
   - To stimulate and motivate clients by developing an interest in horticulture.
   - To help clients socialize and interact with staff and volunteers.
   - To provide an outlet for creativity and imagination.
   - To provide a nonthreatening environment that can help clients adjust to a hospital or new environment.
   - To provide a therapeutic program that can facilitate a wide range of problem areas.
   - To provide a pleasurable experience.
   (See *Year-Round Calendar of Horticultural Activities*).

4. **Referral system**—clients are referred by the treatment team.

5. **Program Criteria**
   - Participants would include those clients who are interested and motivated in learning about plants and gardening and those clients who would benefit by participating in a nonthreatening activity with plants.
   - The time frame for active clients should be maintained within their capabilities and tolerance levels. For clients who may have mental or physical impairment, the time factor should be determined by their individual needs and the severity of the disability.
   - The size of the group depends on diagnosis and functioning levels. For cognitively impaired individuals, group size may be 1 to 3 per group. For high functioning clients, the optimum number is 10 to 12 per group.
   - The program can take place in the greenhouse, at the raised bed gardens, activity room, grow light area, or the client's room.
   - The content of horticultural activities must enhance the clients' physical and mental capabilities and raise their level of accomplishment. There should be correlative horticultural activities concurrent to the season or event, e.g., plant propagation, vegetable gardening, floral design, numerous horticultural crafts.
   - The method of delivery for the program should be through demonstration by facilitators (volunteers, staff, fellow clients, guest lecturers, guided discovery—"hands on approach", a/v aids, horticulture reference material, lecture series).
   - The facilitator should be a horticultural therapist, if available, or other health care staff, volunteers, etc.
   - Evaluation should be by observation, verbal feedback and written documentation. ❧

CHAPTER

# 3

# *Volunteer Involvement Program*

" *O pen your eyes and search for some man or some work for the sake of men which needs a little time, a little friendship, a little sympathy, a little toil. Search and see if there is not some place where you may invest your humanity."*
$\qquad$ – Albert Schweitzer

The Ontario Hospital Association Task Force on volunteer services defines a volunteer as "a person who does something of his or her own free will for which no salary is received. The three-fold purpose of a volunteer service is to supplement the work of the health care personnel which contributes to total client care; to help promote in the community a thorough understanding of the health care facility and its services; and to provide the community an opportunity to meet a human need to give service by helping others."

The key to a successful horticultural therapy program is in volunteer involvement. Volunteers have assisted me in running the horticultural therapy program at the Homewood Health Centre for 20 years. They assist in the transporting of clients to and from the units to the greenhouse. As well, volunteers take part in the gardening activities and provide the valuable support which has helped to maintain a high quality of care for these clients.

For a good volunteer program, there must be a defined process. Volunteers must know the mission statement or goals and objectives of the institution for which they are working. In some hospitals or institutions, they may run or assist in programs. Job descriptions are excellent tools for defining communication between all individuals involved with programs. It is also imperative to have a line of authority or a discipline that is responsible for connecting the volunteer and client's progress and interaction. Most hospitals, institutions or organizations have their own volunteer department or agencies. If no department or agency exists, then it is your job to recruit, train and manage volunteers regarding the scope of their practice and training.

## *Recruitment: Where to Get Volunteers?*

1. Volunteer agencies: Most towns and cities have volunteer agencies, or bureaus. (See **Resources**).
2. Educational institutions: High school, college or university students are a great source of volunteers to work with a variety of populations. With the emergence of co-op and internship programs, students are placed by their schools and must spend a specified amount of time on the job in order to qualify for a class credit. They are evaluated by both the job supervisor and their school. This allows them to learn on the job, while providing them with an enriching experience. University students enrolled in psychology programs spend one semester in the horticultural therapy program learning the approach to using horticulture as a therapeutic medium. They must complete a journal detailing their assignment and interaction with clients. The concerns of this documentation are then discussed as they pertain to helping clients and meeting their goals in therapy. All names and any information shared is considered confidential. This assignment results in a credit towards a degree in psychology. Because this is a wonderful learning opportunity, students often return to take on other volunteer assignments. Also the time spent volunteering provides students with an excellent hands-on experience to add to their resumes.
3. Horticultural societies: Volunteers who have horticultural backgrounds have proved to be excellent volunteers. With guidance, these people, who often have a wealth of experience, make excellent volunteers, assisting and developing programs in institutions and homes for the elderly, providing resources when budgets and labour are limited.
4. Church groups: These groups are primarily composed of women, who possess a great deal of experience in nurturing and life skills. Clients benefit from their warmth, understanding and genuine acceptance.
5. Advertisements through radio, local cable television, newspapers: Most radio and cable television stations offer free spot announcements for community organizations. Newspapers will often do a human interest story in the family section or insert an announcement in the community calendar section. If you have exhausted the free services, consider placing a paid advertisement, although these can be costly. All of these methods can generate interest from the community. This kind of recruitment often inspires people who may have time available and can offer you varied backgrounds to stimulate your clients.
6. Trade or professional magazines: This type of volunteer usually has definite skills or a background in working with people, such as nurses, therapists, teachers.
7. Professional conferences or workshops: Through networking at these events, you can get and share ideas on volunteers and resources.
8. Public relations: By advertising through booths at malls, libraries, universities, etc. Once a year we celebrate Volunteer Week, with handouts and visual displays of our work. This generates a great

deal of interest and focuses attention on what is happening in our community. This form of advertising also promotes a healthy approach to good mental health and physical well-being.

9. Retired staff: With the advent of early retirement packages and the need to maintain a healthy, active lifestyle, these people provide a great service through their experience, energy, time and skills.

10. Former clients or patients: This type of volunteer usually provides you and your client with their personal experiences and knowledge of what has helped them in their recovery and period of adjustment. It is important that this type of volunteer has been discharged for at least six months before returning in the capacity of a volunteer. This time period ensures an honest commitment and a sincere wish to pursue this avenue of helping others.

11. Multicultural agencies: When working with a variety of clients, frequently you will be exposed to different nationalities and cultures. Having volunteers who understand different languages and customs helps to break down the communication barrier and provides a rich experience in comprehending and relating to their needs and concerns.

12. Word of mouth: This is the best form of advertising, through volunteers sharing their positive experience with others. This form of advertising not only benefits the clients but also promotes the institution and the positive environment in which they are working.

## Screening, Interviewing and Training the Volunteer

Successful recruitment of volunteers is through marketing. It should draw the appropriate type of volunteer, thus reducing the number of applicants who must be screened out.

However, while the first step in securing volunteers is in recruitment, the essential elements of volunteer involvement are the interviewing and screening process, volunteer placement, orientation, training, supervision and ongoing evaluation.

### Interviewing

Interviewing the prospective volunteer is similar to interviewing and screening paid staff in that you must choose the best candidate. There must be a job description clearly delineating all qualifications needed and scope of duties required to fulfil the role of the horticultural therapy volunteer. Once the prospective volunteer has passed the initial interviewing process he or she should receive an information package, which should include information about the institution; an application form listing experience, hobbies, etc.; and a job description using the following as an example:

### Job Description

· Position Title: Volunteer, Horticultural Therapy.

· Organizational Relationships: Reports to Director of Volunteers, Horticultural Therapist or discipline through which volunteer is based.

· Position Summary: The volunteer is to assist in the provision of horticulture as a therapy for all clients, and to contribute to the clients' well-being through the medium of horticulture and horticultural related activities.

**Primary Responsibilities**

- Assist clients in all programs of horticultural therapy, i.e., indoor gardening, floral design, seasonal crafts, outdoor gardening and related horticultural activities.
- Provide written and verbal feedback regarding clients' progress. This information is determined through interaction and observation with the client.
- Help clients to socialize and interact with others.

**Scope of Duties**

- Assist with the transportation of clients to the greenhouse or garden areas.
- Help set up and organize project material for client participation.
- Assist the client in developing positive work skills.
- Help maintain the work area, i.e., assist clients in cleanup and general organization.
- Assist the therapist in teaching horticultural skills to clients.
- Be aware of tools (scissors, knives, pruning shears, etc.) and where they are stored.
- Volunteers will assist in the maintenance of the plant areas, i.e., watering and fertilizing plants, plant identification and general care.

**Qualifications**

- Experience working with people and plants.
- Some experience in gardening.
- Knowledge of plants and plant related activities.

**Physical and Visual Requirements**

Volunteers must be able to:

- Escort wheelchair clients to and from the unit.
- Lift and move small plants.
- Walk to the garden area on hospital property.
- Withstand heat and light from greenhouse exposure.

**Working Conditions**

- Greenhouse environment, gardens and grounds, patio areas with plants.
- A minimum of a six month commitment is required for working in this program area.
- The volunteer will be directly under the supervision of the horticulture staff member.
- The volunteer must sign a confidentiality pledge when working with clients.
- Volunteers should have liability insurance.

The volunteer must meet all the essential qualifications in the above categories. During the interviewing and screening process, the candidate should have the following personality characteristics: a positive personality and attitude, respect for others, empathy, be supportive and nonjudgmental.

## Why We Need Volunteers

Due to today's economy and budget constraints, staff cannot perform all the tasks they would like to achieve. This is offset by people volunteering their time and talents. During program sessions, it is a pleasure to have a variety of volunteers available to assist me in my work with clients. You know they are there because of a desire to help and be of support or assistance. This attitude and willingness to be involved is infectious and inspires clients to become committed to their recovery.

Volunteers have a set time or pattern for work, this schedule helps you organize and maintain a consistent program.

When activities require tasks that cannot be done by clients, e.g., picking wildflowers for pressing, volunteers can assist in this chore thus enabling the client to participate in an activity he or she could not ordinarily do.

Often volunteers possess a variety of skills and backgrounds. These assets can be paralleled with individual clients to help build a rapport and set the tone for a positive experience.

Volunteers promote a healthy outlook in the community and break down the stereotypical thinking towards mental health issues or problems. Also, volunteers provide a link to community resources and associations.

## Evaluating Volunteer Involvement

If volunteers are running or assisting in a program, they must have feedback regarding their involvement. This interaction allows for good communication and promotes a sense of caring and credibility. Evaluations should be done on a yearly basis, both formally and informally, by staff, with client input.

Volunteer associations are also assessed by the Canadian Council on Health Facilities Accreditation Standards (CCHFA). ❧

# *Populations and Diagnostic Categories*

The therapeutic dynamics I use as a basis for working with clients is called the "Humanistic Approach" or "Rogerian Theory." It was developed by Carl Rogers, an American psychologist. The emphasis in this theory is that individuals be encountered and understood. The essence of this client-centred therapy is for individuals to help themselves. Rogers believes "in the basic goodness and potential for growth in all human beings."[1] The therapist does not give advice or interpret directly but rather reflects or restates what the client is saying, accepting and valuing the client as a human being. Rogers' remedy is "to provide the appropriate psychological soil in which personal growth can resume; this soil is the therapeutic relationship."[2]

## Populations and Diagnostic Categories
- Schizophrenia
- Depressive Illness/Affective Disorders
- Organic Disorders
- Alcohol and Drug Addiction
- Anorexia Nervosa

---

1. Wrightsman, Singleman, Sanford. *Psychology—A Scientific Study of Human Behaviour.* Brooks/Cole Publishing Company, Monterey, California. 1979, page 8.
2. Gleitman, Henry. *Psychology.* W.W. Norton & Company Inc., New York. 1981, page 728.

The above disorders will be listed within the horticultural therapy program outline. The format in each area will include **Diagnosis or Population**; **Why Horticultural Therapy?**; **Goals and Objectives** and **Special Considerations** when working with these clients. Projects may be listed or found in the Chapter under *Projects*.

## ﾰ Schizophrenia

"A large group of disorders, usually of psychotic proportion, manifested by characteristic disturbances of language and communication, thought, *perception, affect*, and behaviour which last longer than six months. Thought disturbances are marked by alterations of concept formation that may lead to misinterpretation of reality, misconceptions, and sometimes to *delusions* and *hallucinations*. Mood changes include *ambivalence*, blunting, inappropriatness, and loss of empathy with others. Behaviour may be withdrawn *regressive* and bizarre."[3]

### Why Horticultural Therapy?

The Horticultural Therapy Program utilizes horticulture and horticultural-related activities to maintain or maximize a client's optimum level of functioning. Through the nonthreatening environment of the greenhouse, gardens and plant areas, clients can build self-esteem and feelings of independence.

### Goals and Objectives

The work site (greenhouse, gardens and activity room) for all clients should provide a calm nonthreatening area that can help with their adjustment to the hospital. This therapeutic environment sets the tone for the client's success and continued program involvement. Plants used should be colourful and non-poisonous. Plant material that has colour, scent and texture can alter thought disturbance and promote reality. Through bright colour, texture and fragrance, the senses are stimulated and a sense of now and what is happening is validated.

Schizophrenic clients usually spend a great deal of time in hospitals, and a "learned sense of helplessness" can take place. Motivating these clients to attend programs requires supportive attitudes and a sense of caring. This can be achieved by promoting a sense of structure and security through well-organized work areas where plants and related material are easily identified. Working in a group setting with other clients, staff and volunteers results in an increase in positive, interpersonal experiences. Through attending programs, clients build their activity levels, increase attention span and develop appropriate behaviour.

Digging, mixing soil and breaking clay pots into chips provides a practical outlet for anxiety and stress. Plants provide a tangible and physical medium that responds to nurturing and care. The result of growing plants promotes self-esteem and an increased level of functioning. Skills, such as growing vegetables and herbs, enables clients to grow their own food, to learn about nutrition and to help develop good use of their leisure time.

Exercise through horticultural activity, such as gardening and nature walks, promotes physical fitness.

---

[3] Stone, Evelyn M. *American Psychiatric Glossary.* 6th Edition. American Psychiatric Press Inc., 1988, page 149.

## Special Considerations

Know what medication these clients are on, as there are physical and psychological side effects. (See *Medication*). In addition, clients may be allergic to pollen, mould and insects. Provide sunscreen, hats and protective clothing when working outside.

## Projects

Provide a variety of projects to stimulate and motivate your clients. Know your clients' capabilities and limitations. Projects should parallel the time and season and provide a sense of reality. (See *Year-Round Calendar of Activities*).

### Depressive Illness/Affective Disorders

"Affective Disorders are a group of illnesses of variable severity. The central symptom is a periodic alteration of mood into mania or depression, usually accompanied by other characteristic symptoms."[4] Symptoms of mild depressive disorder include phobias, obsessional thoughts, anxiety, and hysteria. Symptoms of major affective disorders, i.e., depression and mania, include: delusions and hallucinations, resulting in impairment of insight and judgment.

## Why Horticultural Therapy?

The horticultural environment provides nonthreatening conditions to alter the client's mood and enhance or rehabilitate emotional well-being.

## Goals and Objectives

Be supportive of your client. Build a caring and optimistic relationship. Determine what your client's mood is so that you can structure your activity to elevate or alter behaviour. Provide an optimum environment to promote a healthy attitude that discourages negative thinking (somatic complaints). Unhealthy plants are used to help clients understand the cause or problem that is affecting the growth of the plant. This type of analysis gives the client an opportunity to look introspectively at problem areas of their own lives. They are then able to arrive at conclusions that can assist them on the road to mental wellness. Use projects that will increase self-confidence and self-esteem. Socialize and interact with clients who tend to isolate themselves from others.

*Cereus* (Night Blooming Cactus)

For clients who demonstrate aggressive energy and poor sleep patterns, provide physical activity, such as digging, hoeing and pruning. Clients who cannot sleep will enjoy and be intrigued by the *Cereus* (Night Blooming Cactus) that opens only at night or *Nicotiana* (Flowering Tobacco) that produces an intense fragrance at sunset. These plants stimulate interest and positive use of time.

Provide multi-dimensional, floral projects (see *Year-Round Calendar of Activities*) to stimulate creativity and imagination. To build concentration and the functioning level of clients with limited attention span, use projects that are challenging and interesting. Short-term projects can yield instant gratification, guarantee satisfaction and an increased sense of self-worth.

---

4. Morgan, H.G., Morgan, M. H. *Aids to Psychiatry*, 3rd Edition, Churchill Livingstone Inc. New York, 1984, page 61

Teach horticultural skills, such as vegetable and herb gardening, to promote good nutrition.

## Special Considerations

For clients who display symptoms of increased irritability, activities such as harvesting vegetables, watering or walking in the garden can encourage a sense of independence and provide some space to deal with these emotions. Clients who have an aversion to working with dirt or soil will find soilless mixes a suitable way to keep their hands relatively clean and decreasing their anxiety level.

## Projects

Projects should maximize clients' capabilities and strengths. Design projects promote creativity and are good avenues for self expression and imagination.

## ⁂ Organic Disorders

## Dementia

"Impairment in short and long term memory associated with impairment in abstract thinking, impairment, judgement, other disturbances of higher cortical function, or personality change. The disturbance is severe enough to interfere significantly with work or usual social activities or relationships with others."[5]

## Alzheimer's Disease

The initial stage is characterized by memory loss that becomes more pronounced with the onset of depression. At the outset of this disease there is loss of cognitive functioning. This includes language, motor skills, recognizing objects, disorientation, severe memory loss, anxiety and agitation. Clients also experience sleep disturbance, wandering, pacing and aggressive behaviour. The terminal stage includes profound dementia, loss of continence and the ability to walk and talk and eventually results in death.

## Why Horticultural Therapy?

The greenhouse or plant environment provides a safe, nonthreatening area for clients to deal with adjustment and reduce agitation. Working with selected herbs and flowers provides a great medium for sensory stimulation (See *Useful Plants for Starting a Horticultural Therapy Program*). With the deterioration of cognitive functioning, horticultural tasks can be modified according to difficulty, in order to measure patient concentration, retention and method interpretation.

A walk in the garden can reduce clients' agitation and alter negative thought processes. Working with plants and flowers can increase attention span and promote skill levels. Horticultural tasks can stimulate work skills and past memories.

## Special Considerations

It is important to know the stages of this disease to determine the functioning level of the client. The activity must meet the client's capabilities. Always use non-poisonous plant material that stimulates response through taste, touch, sight and smell. Adapting the environment is an important factor when working with people who are cognitively impaired. Keep the worksite safe, comfortable and uncluttered; this includes barrier-free areas and adapted equipment for special needs. (See *Adapting Special Tools*).

---

5. *American Psychiatric Association* DSM IIIR. 3rd Edition, 1987, page 103.

Be aware of the accompanying symptoms of this disease; intense confusion, depression, anxiety and isolation. Alter your program to meet this behaviour. Always identify who you are and look directly into the client's face. Tone of voice is more effective than volume. "Listen" with your eyes and ears and speak slowly. Give reassurance through touch, a smile and tone of voice. When working with clients, short statements such as "water the plant" provide direction and help eliminate confusion and decision-making.

Parallel the activities to the season or event. Simple short-term activities are more therapeutic and beneficial than long, repetitive tasks. Know your client's tolerance level and work within the limits of this ability. The most effective way to teach a skill is to demonstrate it through simple instructions.

### Projects
Use real objects or plant materials, such as pine cones, tulips, and fall leaves, to stimulate and validate time of season. Visual aids, such as cue cards that use block printing and large colourful posters are also useful to help clients connect with the task at hand. (See *Year-Round Calendar of Activities*).

### ❧ Alcohol Addiction
An alcoholic is anyone who experiences problems in his or her life as a result of drinking. The problems may be personal, social, physical, economical-occupational or legal.

### Why Horticultural Therapy?
Horticultural therapy offers clients an opportunity to develop positive leisure and coping skills to aid in the recovery process. The goal of recovery is to replace the alcohol with people or other things; assess relationships, healthy or unhealthy, and change life styles by offering a renewed sense of purpose.

### Goals of Horticultural Therapy
Horticultural therapy provides a plethora of activities to stimulate clients' interest and encourage ongoing treatment. It can promote self-esteem and a sense of worth through gardening skills. The environment is substantially more relaxing than that of an otherwise busy and hectic treatment regime. Practical skills are developed that can be utilized after discharge. Quality of time is improved and negative life styles altered. Stress is relieved through a physical or creative activity. Proper nutrition is promoted through the culture of herbs and vegetables. Physical strength is built or maintained through gardening chores

and exposure to fresh air and sunshine. Working with plants is a new learning experience and provides intellectual stimulation. Clients learn to nurture and care for living plant material.

### Special Considerations
During the recovery process, clients may appear physically healthy, but due to the effects of alcohol on the body, the clients' physical and work tolerance may be limited. Be sensitive to the alcoholic's variety of emotions during the recovery process; depression, poor self-worth, guilt and despair. When working with the male population, introduce activities that are nonthreatening, such as vegetable or herb gardening, then work up to more creative tasks to promote a sense of gender security.

**Projects**

If clients are physically healthy, they can perform most horticultural tasks. (See *Year-Round Calendar of Activities.*)

### ❧ Anorexia Nervosa

"Refusal to maintain body weight over a minimum normal weight for age and height; intense fear of gaining weight or becoming fat, even though underweight; a distorted body image; and amenorrhea (in females).[6]

### Why Horticultural Therapy?

Young adults who are admitted to the hospital environment experience confusion and fright. The greenhouse and plant areas provide a safe, nurturing environment to ease some of these fears. During the regimented treatment process for anorexia nervosa this environment provides a sanctuary for clients.

### Goals and Objectives

Horticultural activity stimulates the mind and helps reduce the preoccupation with food or weight. Feelings of self-worth are increased through a positive experience. Group projects in the greenhouse improve healthy behaviour and interaction between staff and clients. Concentration levels increase when an interest in plant material and related projects is established. Personality characteristics, such as moodiness and obsessive thoughts, are altered by ongoing involvement in structured activities.

Growing vegetables for their nutrient value teaches clients how to gain back nutritional elements, such as potassium, that have been lost through vomiting or the use of diuretics. Clients learn to exercise normally through a horticultural activity.

### Projects

Projects must generate a feeling of accomplishment and self esteem. Creative tasks are excellent for exhibiting imagination and self expression. ❧

---

6. *op cit.*, page 65.

# CHAPTER

# 5

# *Chemical Dependency*

T he fragrance of lush, blue hyacinths permeates the warm moist greenhouse air. Large, cascading, purple and green Wandering Jew hangs in rows along the rafters. Bins of rich, black earth and white perlite lodge between benches of tropical plants. These are the sights and sensations that greet recovering chemically dependent clients in the horticultural therapy program.

A person who is chemically dependent is anyone who experiences problems in his or her life as a result of substance abuse. These clients are admitted to Homewood and placed in the Homewood Alcohol and Drug Services (HADS) program. Their problem(s) may be personal, social, physical, economical, occupational or legal. HADS exposes clients to the many therapeutic and leisure aspects of treatment. Horticultural therapy offers an abundance of activities to these clients, to meet individual or group goals and objectives for recovery. Some of these goals include the replacement of alcohol and drugs with people; assess relationships, healthy or unhealthy; and change of lifestyle by offering a renewed sense of purpose.

Horticultural therapy helps clients to discover that through leisure activities, their potential to grow, learn and change, and thereby achieve a more satisfying, qualitative way of life.

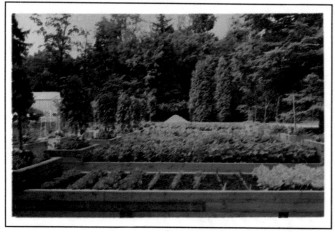

The flourishing greenhouse and garden offer a nonthreatening and safe environment to an otherwise busy and hectic treatment regime. Here, clients master the art of growing plants, talk about their disease and discover the possibilities of how to have fun without alcohol or drugs. Classes in the horticultural therapy program include vegetable gardening, plant propagation, cacti dishes, making grapevine wreaths and numerous other horticultural tasks. Practical skills are taught that can be used after discharge to help improve quality of time and alter negative life styles.

Recovering clients experience a variety of emotions during the recovery process, such as depression, poor self-worth, guilt and despair. Building gardening skills and accomplishing meaningful duties either in the garden or greenhouse assist in building self-esteem and a sense of self-worth. Depression is eased by providing an avenue for expression through creative design classes. Here, in this group setting, clients can talk about their apprehensions with others while participating in a creative outlet that can relieve stress.

Goals in the program are SMART (Specific, Measurable, Attainable, Result-oriented and Timely/trackable), meeting the client's capabilities. One man I worked with was having problems concentrating on creating a pinecone wreath. After a period of time and repeated instructions, he was able to complete this project. He wept and told me that "everyone," including his family, "had given up on him" and this was the first time he had been able to complete and achieve something of worth. Members in the group were also supportive and a sense of caring was evident. Volunteers also aid the people in the program by assisting each individual to achieve positive results and experience healthy feedback and good communication.

Sometimes, working with a plant helps an individual who is an alcoholic to understand a drinking problem.. A client working in the greenhouse was experiencing difficulty in dealing with the fact that she was an alcoholic. She saw this as a social drinking problem and was in denial. I had her purposely overwater a jade plant for a period of time, which eventually became chlorotic and sickly. This outcome enabled the client to see the relationship between the effects of the over-watered plant and her substance abuse.

During the summer months, clients are introduced to work in the raised-bed gardens where we grow many varieties of herbs, vegetables and flowers. .Usually, women are eager to help and to get involved with these garden tasks, whereas men tend to be threatened if the job appears outside of their perceptions of their masculine role. However, once the group gets busy and begins to enjoy the camaraderie, these fears disappear and a more accepting and pro-active attitude takes place. During these garden periods, we talk about how gardening plays an important role in the recovering alcoholic's road to physical and mental health.

Nearly all chemically dependant individuals eat poorly during their dependancy. Although these clients look fairly strong, in fact their physical and work tolerance is somewhat impaired. Alcohol and drug use suppress the appetite and the absorption of nutrients is impaired while the body's need for certain vitamins is increased. Nutrient deficiencies of thiamine and vitamin C result in Beriberi, scurvy, Korsakoff's syndrome and Wernicke's syndrome. Clients learn which fruit and vegetables contain essential vitamins and minerals and how their deficiency can harm the body. This information provides these clients with an understanding of the importance of nutrition in their total rehabilitation. Additionally, their physical strength is enhanced and exposure to fresh air and sun improves their over-all health.

Another dimension to these classes is the nature walks and ecology studies which provide a learning experience, as well as rekindle old feelings and memories associated with nature and happier times. Identifying the different trees and wild flowers becomes a stepping stone for connecting with past events of "where" and "what" each person was doing at some stage in their life. Understanding the cyclical nature of growing can intensify an appreciation of life and also be very spiritual.

Over the past few years, I have found horticulture has had a profound effect on the lives of people in a recovering process. It not only leads to a rewarding lifestyle, but also to a healthier and happier outlook.

Former clients drop off pinecones, grapevines and new plants they have grown and share their positive experiences and outcomes with me. A former client who had a serious alcohol problem, left a stressful job to open up a craft shop as a result of being exposed to the creative design classes. She, indeed, altered her lifestyle and created a new career and life for herself and her family.

I have seen how the program helps the recovering alcoholic regenerate emotionally and find a restored sense of control over the often uncontrollable events of life, without resorting to alcohol and drugs.

Horticulture may not be a cure-all for everyone, but for some it has been the road to recovery and to self actualization! ❧

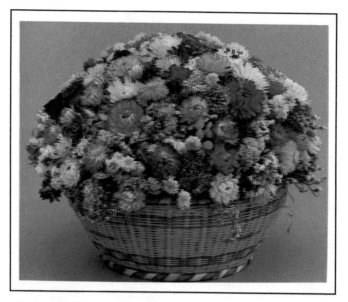

This beautiful arrangement of dried flowers was created by a former client, who gave it to me to show her appreciation for the role horticulture had played in her recovery. She wrote *"...As I was driving around, I noticed all the wildflowers along the roads. I started slowing down and realized how beautiful the countryside was. I was never without my scissors and my "duck boots," always prepared in case I came across something to add to my collection. I often thought about all the times I had driven along these roads and never seen the beauty out there. I guess that is what so many years of drinking and not caring will do."*

# CHAPTER

# *6*

# *Medication*

I t is of prime importance that the horticultural therapist be conversant with the medication clients receive. In many instances drug therapy is part of the client's ongoing treatment. However, many drugs have side effects and conditions that should be recognized in order to prevent or lessen injury. The criteria listed here are not all-inclusive, but are pertinent for horticultural therapists.

The following medication will be listed by name, treatment, possible side-effects or precautions necessary. This information was taken from a list of medication prepared by the Pharmacy Department of the Clarke Institute of Psychiatry, Toronto, Ontario.

## Carbamazepine
This medication is used to treat epilepsy, trigeminal neuralgia and mood disorders.

## Side-Effects
Dizziness caused by moving too quickly, drowsiness, ataxia, blurred vision and skin sensitivity.

## Precautions
Clients taking this medication should not get up too quickly or be involved in strenuous activity beyond normal. Avoid activities that require fine eye-hand coordination, such as planting small seeds and transplanting seedlings, until clients regain visual acuity.

## Neuroleptics

This group of drugs is also known as antipsychotics or major tranquilizers. They are used to treat symptoms of acute or chronic psychosis, including schizophrenia, mania and organic disorders.

### Side-Effects

Drowsiness and lethargy, dry mouth, blurred vision, dizziness, tardive diskinesia (involuntary movement of muscles) and serious sunburn with a little exposure to sunlight.

### Precautions

Avoid fast movement and give clients regular break periods. Provide water or sour candies for "dry mouth" and to prevent dehydration. Those clients who experience involuntary movements of the muscles can perform most garden chores except for fine, detailed tasks. Because a little exposure to sunlight can cause serious sunburn, make sure clients wear protective clothing and use a sunscreen that contains PABA. Garden in the morning. For clients who are injected for long lasting results, do not indulge in physical activities beyond the normal within the 48-hour duration of the injection.

## Clozapine

This is also a neuroleptic (antipsychotic or major tranquilizer). These drugs are used to treat symptoms of acute or chronic schizophrenia in clients who have not had an adequate response to other neuroleptic drugs.

### Side-Effects

Drowsiness and lethargy, dry mouth, drooling, dizziness or fainting, muscle spasms, tardive dyskinesia and temperature reaction.

### Precautions

Avoid warm temperatures that promote sleepiness; provide fresh air and stimulating activities. Have water and sour candies on hand. Do not let clients stand for too long a period, and provide short breaks. Do not work on projects that require fine eye-hand coordination and avoid glass projects (terrariums) when muscle spasms are apparent. Provide good air circulation and avoid hot sun areas that may affect a client's body temperature. Use protective clothing and sunscreen when outside.

## Cyclic Antidepressants

These medications are used primarily for depression and may also relieve anxiety.

### Side-Effects

Dry mouth, blurred vision, dizziness, sweating and muscle tremors.

### Precautions

Avoid exposure to extreme heat and humidity, because the drug may affect the body's ability to regulate temperature.

## Hypnotics/Sedatives
These drugs are used to treat sleep problems.

## Side-Effects
Morning grogginess, restlessness, upset stomach, confusion or disorientation; nervousness, excitement, and behaviour changes; lack of coordination, causing falls and dizziness.

## Precautions
During periods when clients appear groggy and restless, change your activity to provide interest. Allow the client to do a variety of tasks to keep interest peaked.

## Anti-Parkinsonian Agents
This is medication used to treat muscle side-effects some clients experience when they are treated with neuroleptics.

## Side-Effects
Drowsiness and lethargy, dry mouth, blurred vision, nausea or heartburn, disorientation, muscle weakness and temperature.

## Precautions
Avoid high temperatures; provide stimulating activities that do not require fine eye-hand coordination.

## Anxiolytics
This medication is used to treat symptoms of anxiety. Anxiolytic agents are called minor tranquilizers.

## Side-Effects
Drowsiness and lethargy, blurred vision, lack of muscle coordination and slurred speech.

## Precautions
Provide stimulating activities and avoid fine eye-hand coordination tasks.

## Lithium
This is used in the treatment of mood disorders.

## Side-Effects
Marked trembling, loss of balance, slurred speech, abnormal weakness or drowsiness, dizziness, dry mouth, blurred vision, sweating and excitability.

## Precautions
Clients are on special diets to prevent any reaction to this drug. Be aware of all side-effects and act accordingly. ❧

# *The Work Area*

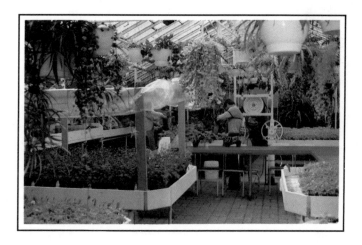

**T**he Greenhouse – The first choice for anyone practising horticulture as a therapy is a greenhouse, because it has the best possible environment for growing plants! It also provides a wonderful therapeutic environment for the clients, because of the openness of the glass walls and ceiling, which give the illusion of being outside, thereby creating an atmosphere of safety. The greenhouse atmosphere, with its moist air and warm sunlight, nurtures a sense of comfort and well-being associated with being close to the earth and nature. At night, the greenhouse gains a different dimension, rich with lush, green colours, scents and moisture.

At the Homewood, a long, glass show window allows visitors, clients, staff and volunteers to see into the greenhouse and classroom area. Displayed in the window are the types of projects and activities that are ongoing in the horticultural therapy program. Many of these projects are for sale. The window is also designed each month to depict a season or event.

This area is adjacent to the coffee shop and because of its openness and light, fosters a sense of well-being and interest in the horticultural therapy program. It also provides good public relations for the hospital environment.

Almost anything can be grown in a greenhouse, if you know the culture and care of the plants. A greenhouse allows you to control your crops under optimum conditions. It is a location where water and soil spills do not need to be cleaned up immediately. There is room to grow straight in flats and space for a large variety of plants of different sizes, and it also provides a place to experience all aspects of these plants, including that wonderfully fresh smell found only in a greenhouse.

**The Solarium**—Solariums can also be used for a horticultural therapy program. Plants can be grown in them and horticultural activities initiated. There are several limitations, however. The atmosphere in a solarium is usually more artificial, because the function of a solarium is usually as a plant showcase where mature plants are displayed in pots rather than being nurtured from seed. In most facilities, the solarium is designed usually as a multi-purpose area for other activities. Solariums are also expensive to build, are often built as an extension of a building, and the light is not as good unless the exposure is southern. Adaptability for wheelchairs or other adaptive devices is frequently limited because of space restrictions. Maintenance is more difficult because the floor surface is not a natural one, e.g., cement, and spillage of water and soil has to be attended to immediately so that it does not serve as a hazard and is not tracked out. Circulation must be provided and there must be some kind of shading available so the plants do not burn. Nevertheless, with some thought and care, they can be adapted for horticultural therapy.

## *Equipping the Work Area*

When equipping your work area you will want a non-slip floor area, preferably with a drain; tables that are at wheelchair height, i.e., approximately 30 inches (76 cm); comfortable chairs with armrests; large containers or bins filled with soilless mixes, perlite and vermiculite; a sink area for cleaning up and an outlet for water; different sizes of watering cans; trays and pots; aprons; cleaning supplies and a broom and dustpan.

### Plant Pots

The piece of equipment you will use the most is the plant pot, and you should have a large range of sizes in stock either in plastic or clay. Plastic pots are an oil bi-product or are made from recycled plastic and are therefore cheaper. But clay, while more expensive, is better for the larger plantings. The one disadvantage of clay is that it has to be scraped and cleaned periodically because of the build-up of white calcium and salts.

Other necessary equipment includes flats and seed cells for growing plant material. I use Rocket Packs. They are wonderful for propagating plants, because they hold 26 plants, are lightweight and inexpensive.

For both indoor and outdoor digging, you will need round-headed shovels, spades, garden forks and trowels. For arthritic hands, I use large, padded soup spoons. You will also need rakes, hoes and appropriate tools for cultivating and weed control. For pruning, quality secateurs with good spring action are a worthwhile investment. You will also need a variety of supports such as stakes, twine for tieing and tags for marking.

Wheelbarrows for moving large loads outdoors are necessary as are lengths of hose. Use a nozzle end with many small holes for an even water spray.

Sharps include a variety of scissors, knives and hedge clippers, should be kept sharpened and locked up when not in use. (See *Adapting Special Tools*).

## *Maintenance*

Good maintenance is an important factor in running programs in any area, whether it be a hospital, institution or activity room. It involves several procedures. The maintenance steps that follow are primarily for a greenhouse, however the basic assumption holds true for any work area.

### Cleanliness

At the top of the list is a clean environment; no matter where you are working, whether it be a greenhouse, activity room or solarium, floors, benches and other work areas should be kept clean, using a mild solution of bleach or some other form of disinfectant to control germs and disease.

### Tools

When using tools, make sure trowels, spoons, scissors, knives, pruning tools and all other equipment used in conjunction with horticulture are cleaned regularly and swabbed with alcohol, so that diseases and other problems are not carried over to the plants. Tools should also be maintained in good working order at all times, so that when working with clients, tools are ready and it is not necessary to stop because scissors are dull or trowels are rusty. Preventing problems is much better than dealing with them; dealing with them is costly and wastes time and energy.

### Infected Plants

Obviously, in maintaining your area it makes good sense not to introduce sickly plants into the work space. In doing so you are only creating more problems. If you are going to look after this type of plant, set aside a special area and call it a "plant hospital", or some other catchy name. But be sure to keep them away from your healthy plants, so you don't spread disease or insects.

### Containing Disease

Whether to use chemicals or, alternatively, natural methods in disease containment is important. Nowadays, people are very aware of the environment and the need for protecting it from chemicals.

Most people prefer natural methods. There are some chemicals however, such as Malathion or Diazinon, which can be safely used in a greenhouse but are hazardous in a solarium or workshop area where ventilation is limited.

**Natural Control**

The best control is none at all! If your plants are clean before they are brought into the work environment you will not have problems. Inspect plants carefully by turning them over and checking the underside of leaves for larva, webs, or deposits of mold, mildew, or evidence of boring insects. Be extremely thorough, and use a magnifying glass when you are not sure. However, even the most careful of inspections can miss larva or infected leaves. Should some of your plants develop problems, the following natural methods can be followed.

One such method is the use of pure soap, not to be confused with detergent. A solution made by dissolving a few drops of soap, such as Sunlight or Ivory, to a litre of water can be used to wash off plants by spraying them with this solution every three to five days to make sure they are clean, i.e., disease and insect free.

Another natural method is the use of sticky pest strips. These can be bought and attached to sticks that can be placed or hung beside the plant. The strips will attract insects such as mealy bugs, aphids, white fly and thrips and can be purchased at most garden centres, some flower shops and through seed catalogues.

A third method, most popular in the home, is using Safer's soap. This commercial product is widely used, nontoxic and effective. It is sprayed on the plant following manufacturer's directions for specific problems. (See **General Plant Care**).

A fourth method in containing insect pests is biological control. This means introducing host insects that will eat the pests. Ladybugs will destroy aphids and for white fly you can use a parasite called *Encarsia formosa*. There is also a predator mite, *Phytoseiulus persimilis*, which is very successful in controlling infestations of red spider mite and spotted spider mite. It will prey only on other mites. (See **Resources**).

**Temperature and Circulation**

If you do not have good air circulation then the air will become stagnant and a breeding ground for insects, mildew, fungus and a lot of other problems. If you have a small solarium, make sure you have fans or an air extractor to keep the air circulating or to remove excessive moisture and heat. If you have a greenhouse, you should have vents that open automatically when the temperature reaches a certain level. You should also have fans that blow through the greenhouse to keep temperatures consistent to the requirements of whatever crop you are growing, or at least at a temperature to prevent diseases and insects from developing. Provide the right amount of humidity by flushing walkways and paths periodically and your plants should flourish. But remember, excessive moisture can cause plants to rot from molds and mildew, while too little moisture and dry conditions can contribute to insect growth.

Prevent extremes of high or low temperatures. Temperatures should be kept consistent. Evening temperatures are generally cooler.

## Light
In order for the plants to be well maintained, good light is essential. However, provide shade when the sun is too strong, with shade and heat-retention curtain or liquid shading paint. (See *General Plant Care*).

## Water Source
Make sure water is not coming through a softener system, as it will contain salt. Access to water should be close by, so it is not necessary to carry or pipe it from a distance.

## Soil Area
Have a storage area set up for your soil, so that clients know where everything is. This area should have bins of sterilized soil. If soil is not to be used, then there should be bins of soilless mix, called Gro-mix, Pro-mix or other trade mixes. You should also have a bin of vermiculite and perlite, which should be kept moistened enough to prevent fine dust from particles escaping into the air (for clients to breathe).

## Fertilizer
Use a water soluble 20-20-20 fertilizer for most plants.

## Pots
These should be kept clean by washing them regularly, using a mild soap solution and rinsing them in vinegar and water in a solution of three ounces (85.2 ml) per litre of water or one ounce (28.4 ml) of bleach per litre of water. Store clean pots under the benches where they can be kept clean and ready for use. Clay pots should be scraped and cleaned to remove any build-up of salts and calcium.

## Prevention
Good maintenance keeps plants healthy, but even the most exacting inspections will sometimes miss problems. Inspect plants periodically, so that you are aware of problems while they are still manageable. Clean up and remove any plants that are sickly. Do not allow dead leaves and flowers to fall and collect, thereby spreading the problem. Choose plants that are hardy and easy to grow. (See *General Plant Care*). Remember to grow a variety of plants suitable for your available light and area.

## Safety
A particularly important aspect of good maintenance is to have locked storage areas where materials used for maintenance can be kept. Bleach, alcohol, whatever chemicals you may use, plus sharp tools can be extremely hazardous to client population. Keep Material Safety Data Sheets (MSDS) for all your products so that you know their content, identity, storage needs, expiry dates, first aid information and fire and explosive hazards. The MSDS sheet is a two or more page document containing detailed

hazard and safe handling information for controlled products. Be sure to know toxicity and exposure levels of all substances, along with emergency and first-aid procedures. Since the passing of Bill 79 in Canada, it is now mandatory in most hospitals and industry that staff and volunteers be aware of all precautionary measures to take. Safety factors are an integral part of risk management. For further information contact The Ministry of Health, Construction Safety, 400 University Avenue, Toronto, Ontario M7A IT7 or Canadian Centre for Occupational Health and Safety, 250 Main Street East, Hamilton, Ontario L8N lH6. For those practising in the United States contact Occupational, Safety and Health Administration (OSHA), Washington, D.C., or look in your phone directory under the County, Government section.

## Fungus Control

Plants are attacked frequently by either pests or disease. Fungus is something that can usually be prevented or cured by a regular monthly application of a fungicide, in powder form, or by spraying through a mister, but be aware that these fungicides are very poisonous and take the necessary precautions.

If you have only a few infected plants, the cost of this treatment can exceed the net worth of the plants, so rather than treating them, discard the plants. If you are growing seedlings or other types of plants, make sure you use No-Damp or other similar products to assist you in preventing fungus growth.

## Pest Control

Know the insects that are infesting your plants. Be familiar with life cycles, so you will know what treatment to use.

The following are some of the insects that are found primarily on greenhouse plants:

### Aphids

These tiny insects form around new growth. They malform and discolour foliage and flowers. Eradicate naturally with Safer's soap or soap solution, or swab with a brush dipped in full strength rubbing alcohol. If you have a large crop, it is better to use chemical solutions such as Malathion or Diazinon, but these are poisonous so follow instructions and use with extreme care.

### Spider Mites

They are very small and suck the juices out of the plant, killing the leaves. They can be identified by the small webs they leave under the plant. Look for them with a magnifying glass, because they are hard to see with the naked eye. They will reproduce if the area is dry and has poor circulation, so make sure you provide moisture and proper cultural conditions. Mites can be treated with a dormant oil or a product that will smother the eggs and kill them. Again, know the life cycle, so that you can destroy the adults as well as the eggs.

## Mealy Bugs

These have soft to hard scales and are brown, black, slow-moving insects. They leave a little bit of white "cotton" and can be treated with alcohol, strong soap, or Malathion.

## White Fly

This insect is very prolific, laying thousands and thousands of eggs. If you tear off a little corner of paper and drop it, you will get an idea of what a white fly looks like. They are little white specks, not much larger than a grain of salt, flying off plants, and nearly all plants are hosts. Spraying with Safer's or a soap solution should be done every three days for a period of two weeks, to break the life cycle which includes the eggs and adults. Malathion and Diazinon will also work.

## Fungus Gnats

Another insect that is prevalent is the fungus gnat. These insects live off decaying material on moist plants. The eggs and adults must be killed in the soil by using either a systemic insecticide or spraying with Safer's, Diazinon or Malathion, all of which are interchangeable. Allow the soil area to dry out between waterings. (For further information see *Resources*). 🐦

CHAPTER

8

# General Plant Care

B ecause the medium you will use when working with your clients is the plant, you want to have healthy specimens to show them. If not, then you are dealing in a medium whose infirmity will add to your clients' depression and overall feelings of malaise.

Plants to be grown in a greenhouse, solarium or window environment are determined by available light sources. These sources are: north, south, east and west light, with variations of these, as in southeast, northwest and so on. Grow plants that are suitable for the available light and you should have healthy plants. The following light conditions and examples of compatible plants will help you to get started.

A greenhouse or solarium should face south for maximum light conditions. During the winter the sun streams across from east to west, giving the best possible light for producing healthy foliage and bloom.

**Southern Light**
This is an excellent light source for a number of plants. Plants that thrive in a south-facing area are:

· *Calamondin Orange* (Dwarf Orange Tree) flourishes in this light and produces wonderfully fragrant blooms and oranges. This plant has dimensions of smell and colour, and seeing the bright orange fruit often stimulates clients to learn how to grow this plant themselves.

- **Succulents** and **Cacti**, of which there are numerous species and varieties, also thrive in this exposure. (See *Combination Plantings*).
- **Hibiscus** is a wonderful tropical that produces large, vibrant, single or double blooms.
- *Coleus* is an annual that can be grown indoors. It is an attractive plant with colourful foliage that is easy to propagate.

## Eastern Light

This is the morning light and is cool and consistent. Plants that like this light are:

- **Ferns** were grown by our grandparents in their cool rooms in an eastern light. There is a saying that a healthy fern rustles when shaken.
- **Begonias** are a large genus of plants that produce beautiful blooms and attractive foliage.
- *Saintpaulia* is a genus which includes African violets and gloxinias, of which there are many species, varieties and cultivars.
- *Tradescantia* (Wandering Jew) also prefers this light. This a pendulous plant with interesting leaf patterns.
- **Ivy** likes the eastern light but it does not like heat.

## Western Light

This is a hot, afternoon light. Extra care is required when watering to prevent wilting and leaf burn. Temperatures are highest in summer so make sure there is proper air circulation. Use screening or a shade compound on greenhouse or solarium glass to reduce glare and lower temperature. Plants that do well in this light are:

- **Cacti** will withstand high light, but protect from hot temperatures.
- *Cissus* (Kangaroo Vine) is a large pendulous plant with rich glossy leaves requiring ample space in which to grow.
- **Bromeliads** are cup-shaped plants that produce an interesting variety of foliage and flowers. Water into the centre of the plant. Protect from hot sun.
- **Hoyas** have a waxy leaf and produce masses of delicate blooms that emit a spicy coffee odour and drip honey or nectar.
- *Sanseveria* (Snake Plant) is one of the hardiest to grow and thrives in shade or sun.
  *Crassula* (Jade Plant) also likes it fairly bright.

## Northern Light

This is a low light, common to most environments. It is a constant, dependable and consistent light. A lower light level can be augmented and supplemented by painting walls beige or off-white to reflect incoming light. Plants that do well in this light are:

- *Aglaonema* (Chinese Evergreen), with its striking mottled leaves, provides texture and is ideal for low-light areas.
- *Dracaena* (Corn Plant) comes in many varieties, sizes, shapes and does well in corners or areas with low light.
- **Philodendron** is another plant that does well in low light. It can be grown as a bushy, pot plant or as a hanging plant. It has many interesting leaf shapes from which to choose.

· **Spathiphyllum** (Peace Lily) is a flowering houseplant that produces glossy green foliage and a delicate white bloom.

Remember to rotate all your plants a quarter turn each week to keep their symmetry and prevent them growing toward the light.

## Watering

This is an important aspect of plant care. Water used for your plants must be at room temperature. Let water sit in an uncovered pail until it reaches room temperature. Water can also be used from a dehumidifier, left over water from a kettle and rain water. Water plants well, so that moisture flows out of the pot. Dump excess water and when the plant has dried out, repeat this procedure.

Remember, some plants such as ferns and hibiscus require constant moisture. Never "pocket" water (water in one area); i.e., moisten from all sides of the pot to ensure a thorough saturation of the soil area. Do not let plants sit in water as this promotes rot from lack of oxygen in the soil area. If a water ring is found on the pot, it has been sitting in water too long.

## Misting

Misting plants produces humidity, promotes a healthy plant environment and deters insect development. Do not mist any fuzzy-leafed plants or begonias. Another method is to set your plant in a saucer with pebbles and water. This way, the water level does not touch the bottom of the pot but evaporates around the plant instead.

## Fertilizer

Fertilizers contains three main elements: Nitrogen for green colouring and stem development, phosphates ($P_2O_5$) for root development and potash ($K_2O$) for flower development and sturdy stocks. Flowering plants require more nutrients throughout the year for growth and flower development. Water the soil area before fertilizing to promote faster distribution of nutrients throughout the soil A general all-purpose 20-20-20, water-soluble fertilizer is appropriate for growing most plants in horticultural therapy programs.

Natural fertilizers available are fish emulsion, bone meal or blood and bone meal. Mix water-soluble nutrients with water and moisten the soil area so that the fertilizer will drain through the pot, then remove excess.

Most flowering plants growing and producing flowers should be fertilized at least twice a month. Green-leafed plants require little fertilizer during the winter months. If growing specialty crops, research the proper fertilizer and growing conditions. For most therapeutic programs, avoid growing exotic plants that require special culture and care. Grow an assortment of plants for clients, to provide variety, and promote success, and result in a wide range of stock for projects and activities. For plants growing in a greenhouse, an inexpensive and efficient method of fertilizing is to use an injector system.

The system (Hozon) uses a brass siphon mixer that attaches to the faucet and accurately siphons fertilizer, allowing you to fertilize plants through a garden hose.

## Soil

Always use sterilized soil. Commercial soil is available ready bagged; add perlite, vermiculite and peat moss to lighten soil for an all purpose mix. (Perlite is a white soil amendment derived from lava rock while vermiculite is obtained from formica).

For most programs, I advise using soilless mixes. It is sold in bales, by the cubic foot. The mix usually contains perlite, vermiculite, peat moss and a wetting agent to allow for the absorption of moisture. Some mixes may contain fertilizer for plant growth. These mixes are excellent for starting seedlings and growing most plants. However, plants grown in this mixture must be augmented with fertilizer. There are several kinds of mixes that are sold under different trade names. (See *Resources*).

For larger plants, such as cacti and succulents, substitute sharp sand for the perlite or vermiculite, or simply purchase cactus soil. This will provide better drainage and will also stabilize the weight of the plant. Horticultural charcoal can be added to any soil mix to promote a healthy medium for growing plants.

## Containers

There are many types of containers for growing plants, such as clay, plastic, basket, porcelain and styrofoam. Choose the pot or container that is the most efficient and cost effective. Clay is a natural medium that is porous, allowing plants to breathe easily. Unfortunately, these pots build up salt deposits which must be leached periodically to eliminate them. Leaching involves running water through the plant so that the salt build-up is washed out. Calcium build-up burns the plant, causing yellow top leaves and brown tips. Clay pots are perfect for heavier plants, like rubber plants, jade plants and cacti, since the weight of the clay supports them.

Plastic pots and seed cells are used for growing most crops in the greenhouse. These pots are economical, lighter, easier to use and come in a variety of shapes and sizes. Plastic pots are great for hanging plants, since they are lightweight and do not dry out quickly. They are good for starting small plants and make transplanting to the next size an easy chore. Clients also find these containers easy to wash and store.

If plants are grown directly into containers made of baskets or porcelain pots, there is no drainage and care is needed in the watering process to prevent overwatering. Be sure to put a layer of pebbles or clay shards in the bottom of the pot for drainage, and provide plastic liners for baskets so that water will not leak out.

## Cleaning Plants

Plant leaves must be cleaned to prevent a build-up of dirt and dust. Dirty leaves look unsightly and contribute to poor photosynthesis. During the morning period, wipe the leaves with a cloth dipped in a solution of warm water and mild soap. Gently brace the leaf with one hand and wipe with the cloth. Then clean again with warm water using the same procedure. There are "leaf shine" products on the market that will spray or coat leaves for a glossy look. Limit use of them to once or twice a year. ❧

# CHAPTER

# 9

# *Plant Propagation*

We have talked about growing plants with regard to their light, water, soil, container and fertilizer requirements, as well as controlling insects and disease. Let us go now to plant propagation, the growing of plants from seed, layering, division, cuttings and grafts.

Obviously, you will be growing plants all year-round in your horticultural therapy program. But the best time to propagate is during the growing season, from early spring to mid-summer. The growing season is usually heralded by an awareness in the late winter months (particularly noticeable in a greenhouse or solarium) of an increase in light intensity and duration, which stimulates growth. It can be observed when plants begin to put out new growth and buds start to appear. The four methods of propagation I use are:

- ❧ Seeds
- ❧ Cuttings
- ❧ Layering
- ❧ Division

Grafting is another method, not necessary to use in most programs, but I advise researching the subject if you're interested. All the methods mentioned can be used in a greenhouse, solarium or window program.

## ❧ Seeds

There are many types and varieties of seeds. Most packages give detailed instructions on depth of planting, space required between plants and the kinds of soil and light that are needed.

Some seeds have a hard coat and need to be scarified, or nicked in the shell so that moisture can penetrate and promote germination. Many kinds of seeds, including anenomes, parsley and some trees, need to be soaked before planting.

When planting seeds, I recommend that you use this medium: half peat moss, a quarter sterilized soil and a quarter perlite. You can also use "peat pots" with this mixture, or you can plant them straight into gro-mix, pre-prepared for planting. "Seed cells" come prepared for planting but are expensive for small programs.

To prevent fungus diseases, use "damp-off" to discourage problems when germination occurs. Damp-off is mixed in water and sprayed on the medium, so the seeds are not disturbed.

Containers should be at least 2 inches (5 cm) deep for most plants; the plant medium should be moist and seedlings should be transplanted when the second set of leaves appear.

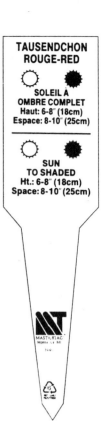

Fertilize with a mild fertilizer, an 8-8-8 ratio, once the second set of leaves appears, at which time seedlings can be transplanted into the three-part soil mixture.

When planting seeds outside, follow the instructions on the back of the seed packet for proper depth and spacing.

Wear gloves when planting seeds that have coatings of fungicide or insecticide.

Water plants from the bottom or provide a mist by using a hose nozzle with a fine spray.

When starting seeds on a window sill or in the home create a greenhouse environment. Cover pots with a sheet of plexiglass or clear glass or use an inverted glass jar or a plastic bag. Do not put seeds into the sunlight. An eastern or morning light is ideal for starting seedlings. Watch for moisture build-up on the inside of the glass, jar or bag, since this may promote rot.

## ❧ Cuttings

Cuttings are one of the most popular methods of asexual propagation. You need a pruning knife, scissors, pots or Rocket Packs, a vermiculite and perlite mixture (rooting medium) and the plants that you will be working with.

The two primary types of cuttings are stem and leaf cuttings. Cuttings are taken from the parent plant. This is the most popular method used in nurseries and greenhouses.

Cut the stem of a healthy plant at an angle 4 inches (10 cm) in length. Remove all flowers and buds to prevent energy expenditure and promote root growth. Remove leaves from the lower 2-3 inches (4-6 cm) of the stem. Leave the top leaves to produce the food required for growth.

Plant the cuttings in sharp sand, or in a vermiculite and perlite mixture. Tamp firmly and keep the rooting medium evenly moist. Plants to use are *Tradescantia* (Wandering Jew), Geraniums, *Coleus*, Impatiens.

When using a rooting hormone that is poisonous, dip the cutting into the liquid or powder and shake off the excess. Be aware that this is a toxic substance.

Stem or cane cuttings can be done on thick stalks, such as *Dracaena* (Corn Plant) or *Dieffenbachia* (Dumb Cane). Cut the stalk from the plant and cut into sections wherever you see nodes. Bury the nodes below the surface of the rooting medium, to produce roots and eventually a new plant.

The second kind of cutting is called a leaf cutting. The plants I prefer to use for leaf cuttings are Begonias, *Sedum pachyphyllum* (Jelly Bean Plant) and *Saintpaulia* (African Violets).

For some leaf cuttings, leave a small portion of the stem and press it into the soil with the leaf facing up, e.g., *Saintpaulia* (African Violet).

Begonias and *Tolmiea menziesii* (Piggy-Back Plant) will produce plants from the leaf. Press the leaf onto the soil so that the underside is against the soil. Cut a notch into the vein(s) of the leaf and keep the rooting medium moist. Where you have made the cut, a new plant will be produced.

*Begonia Leaf Cutting*

### Layering

Through this method of propagation, the stem of the plant continues to receive food and water from the parent plant while new roots are developing. The new plant is cut away from the parent plant and placed in an appropriate soil mixture.

In simple layering, I recommend using *Chlorophytum comosum* (Spider Plant), *Saxifraga sarmentosa* (Strawberry Begonia), *Hedera helix* (English Ivy) and *Senecio mikanioides* (German Ivy). While the plantlets are attached to the mother plant, press the "babies" into a rooting medium and allow two weeks for root formation. Cut off plantlets from the parent plant to form a new plant. Strawberry Begonias, most ivies and hanging plants will reproduce this way.

Air layering is done another way. This is suitable for plants with long stocks that have lost their lower leaves and become unsightly. This method of layering is done to eliminate the long stock and to make the plant more presentable. Dieffenbachias, which are poisonous, can be layered, as can Dracaenas. First, stake the plant so the stem is secure. Notch the stem in a V-shape, a quarter of the way into the stem; this is where the roots will form. Apply a rooting hormone, wrap the cut stem with moist sphagnum moss and then wrap with plastic. Keep this cut stem tied and moist; eventually roots will develop and grow into the moss. Cut off the new plant and plant into a suitable soil mixture.

### ❧ Division

This is the second most popular method of plant propagation. Simply remove the side shoots from the "mother" plant and plant up. The plantlet should be at least half the size of the parent plant. Carefully tap the plant out of the pot and examine it for roots, then pull the "baby" gently away from the "mother". Examples of plants that can be propagated by division are *Saintpaulia* (African Violets), Ferns, Orchids, Bromeliads and Aloe.

CHAPTER

*10*

# *Resource Materials*

For horticultural therapy programs with limited budgets, there are a variety of sources available. Be resourceful. Recycle containers from florists or funeral homes. Health care institutions are a good source for plants, pots and containers (left by former clients.) Ask the cleaning staff to save them for you. Collect empty bleach-type bottles and cut them to make useful scoops. Ask paint stores to keep old wallpaper books for you. These can be used for pressing dried flowers.

Get woven fabric remnants, e.g., burlap, from factories for design projects; interior design fabric sample books can be used for sachets; get yarn or rug wool from factories. The pharmacy can supply you with bottles for making vinegars, small silica gel packs for keeping flowers dry and tongue depressors for use as markers and tools for planting. Do not overlook institutional kitchens! They can supply you with large pickle jars for terrariums, egg cups for Easter designs, fruit juice bottles for vinegars, pop cartons for storing and drying material.

Out-of-doors is also a great source of material. Here you will find cones, nuts, acorns and interesting seed pods, harvest teasel, milkweed pods, oats, bearded barley and fungus (green moss that is growing can be dried and used in floral designs and so can reindeer moss). Bark can be used for designing, e.g., maple and birch and barn board makes good plaques. Always look at materials for their potential use or how they can be adapted for horticultural therapy. ❧

# CHAPTER

# *11*

# *Useful Plants for Starting a Horticultural Therapy Program*

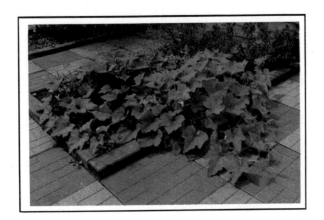

A
t one time, staff at hospitals and institutions grew their own fruit and vegetables as a matter of course. But now, with easy access to fresh produce, and with much larger quantities required, this is no longer viable.  So, with limited space and high land costs, it is imperative that the garden area you choose for your program be: 1) cost effective; 2) produce a bountiful crop; 3) accessible and easy for your clients to maintain; and 4) located in an area with full sun and well-drained soil.  This area must be augmented regularly with rich compost.

Horticultural therapy programs now emphasize the growing of crops that are essential in meeting clients' needs.  For example, growing vegetables is the prime requirement of a specialty program where their cultivation is used to teach good nutrition.  This activity is also a source of needed exercise and encourages the development of a good and profitable use of leisure time.

In this program, different stages in the production of crops provides other diversions; from planting and nurturing, to the process of harvesting them for eating, drying or for their eventual use in crafts and related projects. For instance, growing herbs for their multi-purpose use provides fresh herbs that can enhance the flavour of food; dried and preserved, they can provide material for many projects, such as wreaths, potpourri and vinegars.

Decide with your clients which plants you wish to grow for maximum use. Involve them by asking what they would like to plant; this will provide an essential avenue for commitment, plus a sense of purpose and ownership.

**Harvesting**
Once you have planted and grown your plant material, the key to their successful use is in the harvesting. I do not use any chemicals or dessicant agents because they could be harmful if eaten or ingested.

The most popular method for preserving harvested crops is air drying. It is very successful in retaining a great deal of the natural colour and taste of plants.

Always choose plant material that is in the healthiest condition. Cut stems or flower heads in the early afternoon, after the dew has dried and before they have wilted from the sun. Pick blooms at their peak, except for those that must be harvested in bud stage. When air drying, remove foliage if it is not needed. Secure material in small bunches with elastics or twist ties that will stay tight during the drying and shrinking. Dry most of this material in a dark, well-ventilated area.

Plant material that is to be used in stationery and similar crafts must be dried in a proper flower press, between blotter, or other absorbent paper.

Flowers and foliage will take approximately 3 weeks to dry, depending on the method used, the type of plant and the amount of humidity. After the material has dried, store it in a warm, dry place away from direct sunlight, moisture and dust.

**Therapeutic Applications**
The cultivation of plants provides an avenue for teaching an appreciation of nature's life cycle. Group activities promote socialization and teach clients to work together for a common goal. Planning and organizing a herb or flower garden provides an excellent outlet for creativity and imagination. Digging, pruning and hoeing are excellent opportunities for releasing anxiety and stress in an acceptable manner. Gardening provides clients with an opportunity to build self-esteem through a meaningful, outdoor activity with living material and it stimulates and motivates patients to further this interest when they leave the hospital setting.

Working with selected herbs provides a great medium for sensory stimulation. The older adult responds to most of the scents, colours and textures, as they evoke past memories of food, work skills and special events in their lives. If clients eat the leaves of these herbs, there is no concern about their ingesting a harmful substance. The smell and taste of some of these herbs has a definite calming effect and reduces agitation. The bright colours, shapes and textures of these plants aid clients in cueing and identifying them.

Growing a variety of herbs and flowers can attract butterflies and moths, which adds another dimension to the garden.

## Plant Material

I have found that the following plant material, which gives you an excellent basis for a herb and flower garden, to be the most successful with clients. Most of these crops generally require a full sun area with well-drained soil that can be augmented with rich compost.

*Lavandula* (Lavender)

Herbs: Grow herbs in a sunny area that is self-contained, so that they can be easily labelled, maintained and harvested.

*Menthe* (Mint): Perennial. No gardener should be without this wonderful plant whose varieties include spearmint, peppermint, grapefruit and other exotic flavours. Mint aids in digestion and is great for accenting meat, drinks, ice cream and jelly. The leaves and stalks can be used in wreaths and even as an insect repellent. Fresh or dried leaves make an excellent tea. Contain this plant in a bed on its own since the runner roots can be very invasive.

*Salvia officinalis* (Sage): Perennial. There are over 500 sage species. The wonderful aroma of sage evokes everything from turkey stuffing to aromatic fixatives in beauty aids. The taste and smell of the leaves are a good way to stimulate the senses of clients suffering from dementia.

*Umbellifera* (Parsley): Biennial. Most varieties of parsley are used for garnishing food, in vinegar making, and for flavouring salads and sauces. Parsley contains iron, calcium, thiamin, riboflavin and more vitamin C than oranges. Chewing parsley keeps the breath sweet. Harvest frequently to encourage growth.

*Lavandula* (Lavender): Perennial. It has a comforting fragrance that is calming. The leaves are used in stews, soups, custards and give that distinctive flavour to Earl Grey tea. However, most people are familiar with lavender in sachets and potpourri. Lavender oil is made from crushing the flowers in oil. The mauve flowers are suitable for accenting wreaths, swags and dried arrangements. This plant must be well protected from cold in the winter months.

*Allium schoenoprasum* (Chives): Perennial. The smallest of the onion family, these delicate onion or garlic-flavoured leaves are great in salads, vinegars, sauces and for accenting food. The purple flower heads can be used for flavouring and colouring herbal vinegars, or dried for flower designs.

*Mellissa officinalis* (Lemon Balm): Perennial. A member of the mint family, I use the aromatic leaves for teas, flavouring salads and soups. Use fresh or dried with garlic as a dressing for chicken. The leaves can be dried for a citrus potpourri of dried lemon and orange peel. Lemon balm is used for making tonics and is said to be a very mild sedative.

*Ocimum basilicum* (Basil): Annual. Its glossy, rich green or purple leaves are ideal for giving a peppery, licorice flavour to salad dressings, tomatoes and sauces.

*Allium sativum* (Garlic): Annual. This herb is one of the most popular and widely used plants in the world. It is a major flavour in many recipes, especially in pasta dishes. The stalks can be braided into a lovely kitchen design. Ground up garlic with hot peppers makes a natural bug repellant.

*Pelargonium clorinda* (Scented Geraniums): Perennial. There are over 250 kinds of scented geraniums. These plants are perfect for sensory stimulation. I use varieties with distinctive scents, such as *Pelargonium graveolens* (Rose), *Pelargonium crispum* (Lemon) and *Pelargonium tomentosum* (Peppermint), to evoke a response with patients who have sensory deprivation. The delicate flavours are used in preserves and teas, and they make wonderful sweet pillows and moth bags.

*Thymus vulgaris* (Thyme): Perennial. There are over 100 varieties of thyme. I dry these plants and use them for accenting soups, meat dishes, and vegetables. The flavour of thyme is not as strong if grown in the shade. The small flowers and leaves can be pressed and used in designing floral stationery.

**Flowers**

The following plants prefer a sunny area with well-drained soil that is rich in compost or a natural fertilizer.

*Limonium sinuatum* (Statice)

*Helichrysum bractreatum* (Strawflower): This annual grows to approximately three feet, and is the most popular of the everlasting flowers. The daisy-like flowers range in colours from white, pink, yellow, salmon and rose. Flowers should be picked in the bud stage, before they are fully open. A wire should be inserted through the head before drying. I bunch these together and hang them to dry. The flowers are ideal for all arrangements, especially for table designs, wreaths and swags. For decorative touches, attach as a small bouquet, to a package or container.

*Limonium sinuatum* (Statice): This biennial is grown as an annual, reaches approximately two feet, and its colour range includes white, pink, yellow, lavender, blue and rose. It should be harvested when the colour is showing along the right side of the flower. Hang it to dry in small bunches, in a dark, well ventilated area. The long stems give colour to tall designs and the small heads can be grouped for wreaths. Cut off the delicate flower heads and use them for colour and filler for potpourri.

*Delphinium ajacis* (Larkspur): This annual grows to approximately two feet and its colour range include white, pink and violet. Larkspur dries beautifully and should be hung to dry in bunches in a cool, dark area. Its paper-like blossoms are one of the best flowers to use when designing stationery, candles, bookmarks and floral pictures. I have also seen larkspur and other flowers designed on lamp shades and glass.

*Gypsophila paniculata* (Baby's Breath): A perennial, baby's breath grows to four feet and provides a drift of white when in bloom. The long branches should be separated and hung to dry. The tiny, white flowers give a light, airy effect to most designs and makes a great filler. Baby's breath is a must when creating Victorian or period designs.

*Rosa* (Rose): Perennial. This shrub grows in a range of sizes. Use whatever cultivated variety you like. The flower heads can be hung and dried, or you can separate the petals and dry them in open boxes or on screens. Roses are used in many floral designs (fresh or dried) in bouquets, corsages and in wreaths, baskets and swags where they will provide colour and a focal point. Rose fragrances are often used in beauty products. Rose hips are high in vitamin C and can be used in teas and for flavouring certain dishes. Rose petals are one of the favourite materials for dry and moist potpourri.

*Viola tri-colour var. hortense* (Pansy): This annual grows approximately 6-9 inches tall. It has beautiful, velvety-looking, multi-coloured heads and is familiar to most clients. Grow pansies in window boxes and raised containers for easy access and harvesting. The heads can be dried between blotter paper in a flower press (3 weeks.) Pansies can be used with other flowers in designing shadow boxes, pictures, sun catchers, stationary and numerous other craft items.

*Achillea filipendulina* (Yarrow): Perennial. This plant grows to 4 feet tall. Dry it in bunches in a dark, well-ventilated room. The vibrant, yellow heads are ideal in most arrangements for filling in large spaces and for live design. Heads can be separated into small bunches for fine detail.

*Lunaria* (Honesty): Annual. (Money Plant). This biennial grows up to 4 feet in height and this unique species is already dry when harvested. I sow the seeds in summer for next year's yield. Cut the stalks in late summer before there is a great deal of rain, as they tend to turn black from too much moisture. Remove the outer portion from the pod and you will find an opaque, silver, dollar-like head. The branches are ideal for vase material, or use the outer portion of the pod for making flower heads.

*Nigella damascena* (Love-in-a-Mist): This annual grows up to 2 feet in height and its delicate flowers come in a variety of colours such as white, blue, pink and violet. Flower heads can be dried using a flower press, but the main use for this plant is for the seed heads that form in mid to late summer. Stalks should be hung to dry in small bunches in a dark, well-ventilated area. The pink to rose-coloured heads add depth and beauty to any design.

*Hydrangea* (Hydrangea): (Perennial). This shrub grows up to 5 feet and produces pink, blue or white coloured, flat or cone-shaped flower heads. They must be cut when the flower heads are fully developed. Trim to desired length, remove all foliage and tie into small bunches. Hang the flower material to dry. Big heads can be used for large wreaths and designs requiring bulk or filler. Flower heads can also be cut into pieces and dried in a flower press. Smaller flower heads are used for projects such as notepaper with pressed flowers, placemats and candles. ❧

# CHAPTER

## 12

# *Raised Bed Gardening*

Raised beds for ease of planting have now made gardening possible for those with physical challenges. For individuals who like to garden but are no longer capable of the strenuous labour involved, raised beds allow them to enjoy the benefits of gardening without difficulty.

When I started my career as a therapist in the seventies, most hospitals and institutions had typical vegetable gardens located on flat areas away from the buildings. Homewood was similar in that there was plenty of garden space, but the location prevented direct access. The older adult population and clients with physical limitations were either restricted in what they could do, or unmotivated to work in the garden. Stimulating clients to garden, work in the hot sun, dig, bend and weed took a great deal of encouragement and persuasion. Transporting clients to the garden was a chore, let alone carrying hoses and tools to do the work. Clients had to beware of exposure to the sun because of medication or allergies. Yet, somehow, despite all of these negatives, we managed to get people out to garden and to enjoy this activity. For those who could not get to the garden, the produce and plants were brought to them for their enjoyment.

Today, when I think of gardening this way, I cannot imagine how we managed without raised bed areas, which have eliminated some of the hindrances related to plot gardens.

**Building and Maintaining an A-Frame Raised Bed Garden**

In the early eighties, we decided to develop a plan to change this. Areas were carefully chosen to provide two types of raised beds: one that would be portable, could be stored in the winter months and moved when necessary; the other a permanent site. It would consist of not only raised beds at varying heights but also an area that could support fruit trees, be used as focal point for other activities for clients and staff, and be used from early April to October.

The first site chosen was a patio area located near the older adult clients' residence. There was an access door out to a large patio area that received west sunlight from noon on. Trees provided shade and air circulation. Morning sessions were cool because of shade from the surrounding buildings. Another important element was the availability of water at an outlet located close by. This area was surrounded by a black iron fence that was suitable for suspending flower boxes. A perfect location for a patio garden. When clients learned they would have flowers, vegetable and herbs growing outside their residence there was great excitement.

The ground area was paved with patio stones and grates located off to the sides provided excellent drainage. We asked the clients what they wanted to see in this area and their response was flowers and fresh vegetables, especially tomatoes. The area now consists of an A-frame; table gardens that have

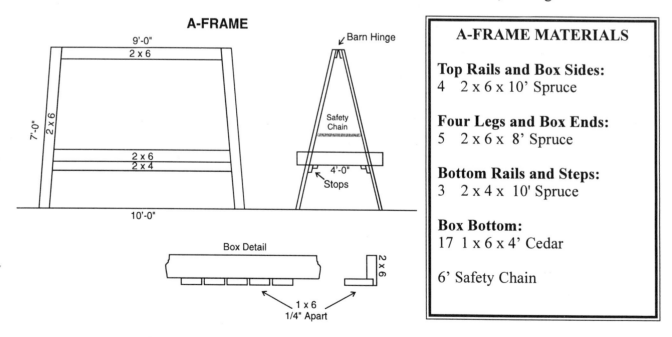

legs and casters for easy movement; eight flower boxes; large, three-tiered wooden plant stands; and eight 10-gallon black plastic tubs. We filled all of these containers with a soilless mix (peatmoss, perlite, vermiculite and a wetting agent). The plant stand was used for a variety of hanging plants, such as lemon ivy, purple heart and geraniums. This was placed in the middle of the patio area to give colour and a focal point. Clients determined the type of plants they wanted to see growing in the containers, and I selected varieties most suited to container growing.

The A-frame, raised planter box and table top beds were easy to plant because of their height. This area provided us with most of our salad crops and were easy to maintain and harvest.

## Successful Vegetables

Lettuce: There are many varieties to choose from, but I use 'Tom Thumb' which is great for confined areas and produces small heads that mature fast, 'Red Salad Bowl', a red leafy crop and 'Iceberg'.

Radish: Use red globular varieties, known as cherry belle or scarlet globe. Mix the seed together with carrot seed, and plant. The radish comes up fast and shows you where your carrots are going to be.

Carrots: Use a short-rooted kind such as 'Orbitt' or 'Kundulus', because of the limited depth of containers.

Beans: Plant French beans, a bush variety that is prolific and a great snack in the garden; provide visual variety with 'Masterpiece' green bean, 'Kinghorn' wax yellow bean, 'Royal Burgundy' purple bean.

Green Onions: Try 'White Lisbon', used in salads, or 'White Spanish', which has a large round shape and is used for slicing. I remember planting onions with a client who had been a farmer for most of his life. He told me "there is no such thing as 'retired' farmers, but rather 'tired' farmers." This client taught me how to plant green onions. I was planting them below the soil line. He told me that it was not necessary to bury them but rather push then gently into the soil, so you could see the top of the bulb. That summer we had the earliest and best green onions ever.

When this A-frame bed was planted, we completed the area with pots of hanging strawberries that hung on large cup hooks suspended from the beam of this garden. This provided a wonderful taste sensation during the early summer.

The black plastic tubs provided us with crops that needed depth and height to grow. Before we planted each container, a brick was placed in the bottom to promote drainage and to prevent the pot from falling over from wind or heavy top growth. The tubs were then filled with soilless mix, the plant staked and tied loosely with a string or twist tie.

The following plants can be successfully grown in 10-gallon containers:

Tomatoes: Try 'Sweet 100' or 'Tiny Tim' tomatoes. Although the tomatoes are small, they make up for their size with their bountiful yield and flavour.

Sweet Green Peppers: For an early, abundant crop that does well in a container, plant 'Canape'. Peppers are generally slow to start, but once they "feel" the warm sun they will grow rapidly.

Beans: Scarlet runner beans have to be staked, or planted beside a trellis. Be sure clients wear gloves if the seeds are coated with a powder. (The seeds are treated with a fungicide to prevent diseases and to promote germination).

Cucumbers: 'Patio Pik' cucumbers are excellent for containers and small spaces. They germinate fast and must be staked..

Swiss Chard: This wonderful, green-leafed plant is hardier than spinach and provides fresh rich greens throughout the summer and fall.

The flower boxes were planted with pansies, lobelia, herbs and scented geraniums that provided colour and fragrance to the area.

## Maintenance

The above crops were easily maintained by clients and staff. Regular classes were held three time a week. All containers were watered once or twice a week depending on the weather and dryness of the soilless mix. Plants were force fed with a water soluble fertilizer (20-20-20) once a week. They received water and fertilizer in the mornings, to prevent mildew and other fungus infections. Always use sterilized soil when planting in a container, to guard against future problems.

Routine inspection and ongoing maintenance will safeguard against insects and disease. If insects appear, spray with a Safer's soap or a mild solution of soap and water, which will correct the situation.

Clients maintain this area doing routine chores including weeding, aerating, removing the side shoots from tomato plants, harvesting crops as they mature, and picking and drying flowers throughout the summer.

## Why Use Raised Beds for Gardening?

This area provided an oasis for clients who otherwise could not garden. They could not go to the garden so the garden came to them. It enabled most clients to garden from a sitting or standing position, providing good range of movement and needed exercise. The patio garden encouraged clients to get out into the fresh air and sunshine.

This activity improved self-esteem and restored confidence. For most older adults this brought back memories of their own gardens and stimulated old work skills. While working here, clients improved their abilities to socialize and interact with other clients and staff, and were rewarded by being able to eat and share the fruits of their labour.

They were able to work independently and use problem-solving skills to deal with the ongoing care of their garden. This area provided responsibility and a meaningful activity for clients. It also furnished a weekend activity with the necessity to maintain the garden area. Another bonus was the pocket of beauty this garden gave to the hospital, and the area of quiet it provided for those who wanted to relax.

The patio garden restored hope and a sense of purpose to those individuals who otherwise would have isolated themselves and not become involved. And most important of all, it was fun.

## Permanent Raised Beds

The second raised bed area we established consisted of permanent raised beds and a gazebo. This area was chosen for many reasons: the space had been our former vegetable area. It was large and provided a full sun exposure. Although the water source was some distance away, it was piped to the garden through underground pipes. The area bordered a road, which meant easy access and the land could also be used for growing other crops, such as fruit trees, herbs and perennials. A neighbouring bush area and nature trail was also incorporated as part of the garden. A large barn was available, with storage space to store our equipment and horticultural supplies.

Consultation with a local landscape architect resulted in a collaborative effort in the design of the raised beds.

There are three important factors to consider when designing a raised bed area:
1) Who, and how many people will be using this area?
2) What special features will make this area accessible and inviting to the clients?
3) What plants will the clients want to grow?

" The older adult client is often afraid of falling; therefore, it is important to provide nonslip, flat surfaces for safety and ease of walking. This will encourage wheelchair clients and those individuals who have canes or walkers to use this area with a sense of security and comfort.
" Good lighting, for evening periods, is essential for safety and the prevention of vandalism. The use of soft, nonglare colours on surface areas subdues harsh and intense sunlight in the daylight.
" Raised beds at various heights will allow clients who have physical limitations to garden from a standing or sitting position.
" Provide lower raised beds, consisting of a square area boarded by 4 x 4 pressure-treated wood, to encourage clients who can bend to get their full range of motion and exercise in the garden. This type of enclosed bed controls herb plants and prevents them spreading into other bed areas. Plastic frames can be used to cover the soil, to warm the earth for early spring planting and to prevent frost damage.
" Water outlets and hoses should be attached to raised beds to provide easy access and ease when watering.
" All raised beds must be insulated with styrofoam to help prevent roots from freezing during early spring thaws.
" There must be a shaded area for protection against the sun, e.g., a gazebo or shade trees. Be aware of clients' medication and allergies to the sun. (See *Medication*).

" There should be a storage shed close to the garden to provide easy access to tools and supplies.
" Provide benches and seating areas for rest and relaxation.
" Determine what type of garden you wish to grow, perhaps one that will promote scent, or continuous bloom or colour. Maintain ongoing interest during winter months, use plants or trees whose leafless shapes will provide interesting silhouettes and colour, such as *Cornus alba* (Red Dogwood), *Corylus avellana Contorta* (Corkscrew Witchhazel and *Salix alba 'Chermesina'* (Willow). Also, choose plant material that can be used for future, related projects. (See ***Useful Plants for Starting a Horticultural Therapy Program***).

To promote ownership and ongoing maintenance, clients should have the option of having their own beds to care for. Work areas should meet the physical and mental capabilities of the client.

Areas that are breezy or experience prevailing winds are ideal for crops that emit fragrance or scent. Depending on the type of client, fountains and bird baths can bring a positive or negative element to the garden. Be careful though, water sounds can promote toilet habits. Poorly maintained bird baths or fountains can promote disease or unsanitary conditions. The sound of wind chimes or fragrant plant material are good auditory and olfactory stimuli for coding the area; that is, clients can smell lilacs or hear chimes and know where they are.

The raised bed area should be bordered by a thick hedge or fenced to outline the perimeter of the garden area. This provides safety for the clients and prevents them from wandering away as well as acting as a deterrent to vandalism.

## Building and Maintaining a Raised Bed Garden

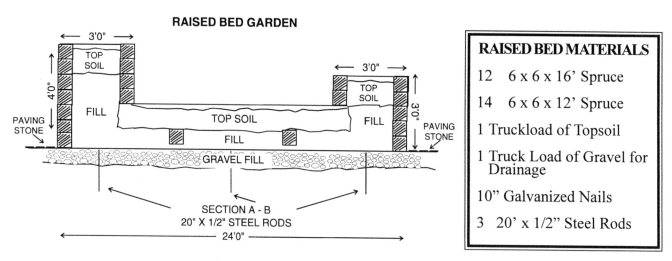

**RAISED BED GARDEN**

| **RAISED BED MATERIALS** | |
| --- | --- |
| 12 | 6 x 6 x 16' Spruce |
| 14 | 6 x 6 x 12' Spruce |
| 1 Truckload of Topsoil | |
| 1 Truck Load of Gravel for Drainage | |
| 10" Galvanized Nails | |
| 3 | 20' x 1/2" Steel Rods |

This plan can be adapted to whatever size you wish to build. Raised beds should rest on a bed of gravel 8-10 inches (20-25cm) deep to provide good drainage. The permanent raised bed area should be located in a full sun area for maximum results.

Fill raised beds with tested top soil. You can test the soil yourself, with a pH kit available at most nurseries and garden centres. If you want this to be done professionally, send a soil sample to an agricultural college or private soil testing lab for testing.

Maintain raised beds with regular fertilizing. Organic fertilizer should be spread 10 pounds (4.5 kilos) per square yard (metre). Mix organic fertilizer, such as sheep or cattle manure, in the soil during the early spring or late fall. If these fertilizers are not available, use well-rotted compost material and work thoroughly into the soil. Augment soil with a soilles mix to keep soil light and easy to aerate.

These beds must be watered every 7 days to keep plants healthy and prevent plant stress that can lead to poor crop production or harvest.

Remove weeds with a cultivator, dutch hoe or by hand to prevent them from taking valuable nutrients and moisture from the soil.

Mulch plants in the summer to provide nutrients, prevent moisture loss and reduce weeds. I use a mixture of soilless mix and organic fertilizer. Spread this mixture between rows of plants; cultivate into the soil and water.

Rotate crops so that you are not draining soil or nutrients and promoting disease and insects by planting the same crop every year. Plant a different crop in each raised bed (over a 3 year period) to promote a good harvest.

Plant crops for harvesting at different time periods to allow for the organizing of work schedules.

When planting seeds, follow directions on the package. The size of the seed determines the depth at which it is to be planted. To make seed planting easier, use seed strips which can be rolled out along the rows. (Available at McKenzie's). (See **Resources**).

## Plant Material for Raised Beds
Raised beds should have a variety of plants to stimulate interest, vegetables and herbs for culinary and project use and flowers for decoration and beauty. If beds are big enough to accommodate small trees and shrubs, choose varieties that are multipurpose, providing fragrance, shade, interesting bark or berries, edible fruit and for the attraction of birds and butterflies.

## Successful Vegetables
A well-planned, raised garden should have vegetables that produce the most nutrients for the least amount of space. The following is a list of plants I have found the most successful:
Tall Crops: Sunflowers and tomatoes.
Medium Crops: Peas, beans, spinach, lettuce, cabbage, peppers and herbs (See **Useful Plants for Starting a Horticultural Therapy Program**).
Root Crops: Beets, carrots, garlic, onions, potato and radishes.
Vine Crops: Cucumber, snow peas, runner beans, squash, pumpkin and melons.

Most of these crops are sown directly in the garden, except for tomatoes, sunflowers, peppers, cabbage and melons, which were started earlier in the greenhouse.

Root crops can generally be planted in early May; tender crops such as peppers, tomatoes, cucumbers, melons and beans, require the warm sun and may die if exposed to an early frost.

## Flowers for Raised Bed Containers

Although there is a great deal to choose from, I grow only those flowers the clients want grown; otherwise, plants are chosen for a particular reason. Flowers should be grown for multipurpose use, to promote colour and enhance the area, and to be used in fresh or dried floral design projects. Plant tall varieties in lower beds for ease of cutting and maintaining. Shorter varieties should be cultivated in higher raised beds, for ease in harvesting. ( See **Useful Plants for Starting a Horticultural Therapy Program**).

## Perennials

*Echinacea* (Purple Coneflower)

*Aster salignus* (Michaelmas Daisy): This tall plant provides a variety of pink and lavender colours from mid-summer well into the fall, after many flowers have withered. The flowers suit fall arrangements and the petals can be used for potpourri.

*Astilbe* (False Spirea): Its soft white, pink or red plumes are ideal for drying and can be sprayed.

*Dianthus* (Pinks): These plants have delicate blooms, are hardy, and will flourish in most soil conditions. The soft range of pink and white colours emit a delicate fragrance and are suitable for small vases.

*Echinacea* (Purple Coneflower): The large, daisy-like flowers are a nice cutting flower, the petals can be dried for potpourri, and the cone-head is ideal for dried flower arranging.

*Echinops* (Globe Thistle): Cut the blue head before the blooms are fully open. When arranged in a container, they provide a beautiful display on their own.

*Liatris* (Gayfeather): This tall perennial gives the garden tall purple spikes that add dimension and colour. The lavender stalks are ideal for drying. Cut once the flower heads open, and hang upside down to dry.

*Limonium* (Sea Lavender): This plant produces delicate purple blooms. Cut flowers before they are fully open for use as an everlasting flower.

*Physalis* (Chinese Lantern): A low raised bed is ideal to grow these plants, since the underground stems spread rampantly and must be kept in check. The flowers are small and uneventful, but the fall turns the paper capsule in which the fruit are located, into orange lanterns. They are ideal for use in wreaths and swags.

*Salvia* (Perennial Sage): This plant produces medium sized, bluish-purple flower spikes that can be dried for arrangements.

*Stachys* (Lamb's Ears): This plant grows to approximately 12-18 inches (30-45 cm) tall. Silky-grey foliage can be dried and used as a base in most floral arrangements.

## Annuals

*Amaranthus* (Love-Lies-Bleeding): This wonderful plant should be planted alone or in the centre of a flowerbed. The unusual red, purple or green, pendulous flowers look like long chenille stems. The flowers dry easily, and are used in dried flower arrangements.

*Celosia:* The cultivated varieties of the species *C. plumosa* produce plumes that add colour and dimension to a sunny garden. The flower heads can be dried and used as filler in most designs.

*Senecio cineraria* (Dusty Miller): The grey, velvety foliage can be dried and used as a base for table and wreath designs.

*Erica* (Winter Heather): This delicate-looking plant produces mauve or pink flowers that can be pressed, with foliage attached. Use in stationary and candle designs.

*Nicotiana* (Flowering Tobacco): This plant emits a small trumpet like flower that produces a strong perfume in the evening.

*Scabiosa* (Sweet Scabious): (Also a perennial). The cultivated variety called 'Paper Moon' produces a round flower that dries into a bronze colour when left on the plant.

*Salvia* (Sage): The variety 'Victoria' produces ethereal-looking stems of purple flowers that dry easily and are ideal for design work in wreaths.

*Lathyrus odoratus* (Sweet Pea): This old fashioned flower is grown for its wonderful fragrance. Grow this plant on a chicken wire fence for support and easy cutting.

*Grasses* (Ornamental Grasses): These plants are a must to grow since they provide you with an abundance of material for dried flower design. There are many species, varieties and cultivated varieties, offering a range of shapes and sizes, that can be either sprayed or dyed. I use them in almost every design piece, for line, filler or colour.

## Trees

Ornamental trees and shrubs are grown in the end of the raised beds for a variety of uses.

*Morus nigra* (Weeping Mulberry): This species should be located at the end of the raised bed to create interest, fruit for making jam and for attracting birds.

*Prunus* (Flowering Cherry): The plants of this genus provide white or pink blossoms that contrast with foliage, providing colour and fragrance in the spring. These branches are forced into bloom during the month of February.

*Prunus erecta* (Flowering Almond): The branches of this species produce a profusion of pink blossoms in the spring and are ideal for forcing in the winter months.

## Shrubs

*Euonymus alatus* (Burning Bush): This deciduous bush, turns completely red in the fall. The stems have a square, cork-like structure that provides a striking line or accent in designs.

*Euonymus japonicus:* An evergreen, is grown for its beautiful foliage, which is ideal in fresh flower designs . I start cuttings in a block of wet oasis and root them for small terrarium plants or grow them as indoor plants.

*Cornus* (Dogwood): The species of this genus provide the raised beds with beautiful colour throughout the year. Spring brings the delicate flowers, summer and fall offer prominently variegated foliage, and winter shows off the stems of the red and gold varieties. I bundle the stems together and wrap them with wire to create a small broom effect. Once they are dried, they can be designed like miniature "brooms."

*Hydrangea:* The large flower heads are a must to dry in the late summer. They can be used for many types of design pieces, and are ideal for a "French country" or Victorian look.

*Forsythia* (Golden Bells): What would spring be without this wonderful shrub? I dry the flowers in a flower press and use them for designing on stationery. It is also ideal for forcing.

*Philadelphus* (Mock Orange): Its flowers produce a sweet aroma and can be pressed for use in crafts.

*Potentilla* (Cinquefoil): The golden or white flowers of this genus can be pressed for crafts.

## Maintenance

Maintain raised beds with regular fertilizing. Organic fertilizer should be spread 10 pounds (4.5 kilos) per square yard (metre.) Mix organic fertilizer, such as sheep or cattle manure, in the soil during the early spring or late fall. If these fertilizers are not available, use well-rotted compost material and work thoroughly into the soil. Augment soil with a soilless mix to keep soil light and easy to aerate.

These beds must be watered every seven days to keep plants healthy and prevent plant stress that can lead to poor crop production or harvest.

Remove weeds with a cultivator, dutch hoe or by hand to prevent them from taking valuable nutrients and moisture from the soil.

Mulch plants in the summer to provide nutrients, prevent moisture loss and reduce weeds. I use a mixture of soilless mix and organic fertilizer. Spread this mixture between rows of plants; cultivate into the soil and water.

Rotate crops so that you are not draining soil of nutrients and promoting disease and insects by planting the same crop every year. Plant a different crop in each raised bed (over a 3 year period) to promote a good harvest.

Plant crops for harvesting at different time periods to allow for the organizing of work schedules.

When planting seeds, follow directions on the package; the size of the seed determines the depth at which it is to be planted. To make seed planting easier, use seed strips which can be rolled out along the rows. (Available at McKenzie's). (See ***Resources***).

## Summation

Raised beds can bring a great deal of pleasure and satisfaction to clients. The beautifully landscaped beds and gazebo area at the Homewood are enjoyed daily by residents, family members and staff. This area provides a pocket of beauty that is maintained by clients. It is close to a bush area and attracts birds and butterflies, creating interest and movement in the garden. The gazebo compliments the area by providing shade and and a place for relaxation.

The overall effect of this garden helps to lessen depression and alter negative emotions. 🙖

# CHAPTER

# *13*

# *Poisonous Plants*

*Croton*

The following popular pot plants are given frequently as gifts because of their foliage, flowers and distinctive fruit. However, they should *not* be used where clients are cognitively impaired, suffer from any kind of dementia, are confused, or where there are little children.

The toxicity levels of these plants vary with plant maturity, part of the plant, e.g., leaves, flowers, berries or bulb and body weight of the person affected.

## Indoor
*Dieffenbachia* (Dumb Cane): If the leaves are eaten, the mouth and tongue will swell, resulting in difficulty in swallowing and speaking. It causes irritation of the mucous membranes when ingested.
*Euphorbia, Poinsettia* (Crown of Thorns): The nectar of the crown of thorns flower causes stomach irritation. The milky sap from the leaves and branches is an irritant and in some cases it can be carcinogenic. *Poinsettia* which is in the same genus, also has milky sap, but when the flowers are eaten there is not the same effect. If you are in doubt, however, do not introduce the plant.
*Lantana*: It is also very toxic. All parts of the plant are poisonous and eating the green berries is fatal. There is stomach and intestinal irritation, circulatory collapse and then death.

*Hedera helix* (English Ivy):  It is toxic if eaten, resulting in excitement, difficulty in breathing, and then a coma.

*Oleander*:  All parts of the plant are toxic, producing dizziness, drowsiness, increased pulse and nausea.

*Solanum pseudocapsicum* (Jersulem Cherry):  The orangey-red fruit will kill an adult if eaten.  It causes stomach pains, low temperature, circulatory and respiration problems, loss of sensation and then death.

Spring Bulbs:  Crocus and daffodil bulbs are both exceedingly toxic.  Eating them causes vomiting, diarrhea, trembling, convulsions and death.

*Croton*:  The milky sap from the stem can cause skin irritation.

## Outdoor

These are plants you should watch for out-of-doors:

*Digitalis* (Foxglove):  Although it is a lovely plant to grow in the garden, be aware that it contains glyceroids which are used as a heart stimulant.  The dried plant can also be lethal to livestock.

Ragweed:  It can cause allergic reactions in people who are sensitive to it. In some areas it has been declared a noxious weed and must be eradicated.

*Larkspur* (Delphinium):  The entire plant is highly toxic if eaten, causing nausea, cramps, bloating, twitching muscles, and paralysis that results in death.

Rhubarb: The leaves cause abdominal cramps, internal bleeding, convulsions, then death.

*Ricinus* (Castor Bean):  Eating two to four seeds could be serious and cause death. Symptoms are burning of the throat and mouth, nausea, stomach pains, thirst, convulsions, uremia and death.

*Convallaria* (Lily-of-the-Valley):  It contains cardio-activity properties, which affect the heart if eaten. All parts can induce an irregular heartbeat, nausea, circulatory collapse and death.

*Taxus* (Yew):  These are often found in foundation plantings of shrubs. The foliage and berries are toxic, causing difficulty in breathing, heart failure and sudden death.

*Rhus radrans* (Poison Ivy):  Its three-pointed leaf can cause severe skin irritation and blistering, which should be treated immediately.

Mushrooms:  Do not eat any mushroom unless you are absolutely certain it is nonpoisonous.  When working with clients, the best protection is to avoid them completely!

*Outdoor Plants/Harmful or Posionous to Humans.* Print Media Branch, Alberta Agriculture, 7000-113 Street, Edomonton, Alberta, Canada T6H 5T6. ❧

# CHAPTER

# *14*

# *Grow Lights*

U nfortunately, most institutions or health care facilities do not have the advantage of having a greenhouse, solarium, or even areas that have access to good sources of natural light. The answer to this dilemma is to provide artificial light by using light stands or grow light units. Most garden centres, plant stores and nurseries carry a variety of light units and structures that can be adapted to most areas. There are even grow lights that fit over a bed or wheelchair (Floralight).

Grow lights will augment your program, and provide you with proper artificial light, so you can grow plants for many activities, on a year round basis. Timers can be added to the units to ensure plants get the proper periods of light, thereby reducing staffing time in maintaining them. It is also important for the therapist to be aware of the plants' response to light and diagnose any problems that might arise. This knowledge should be passed on to clients caring for these plants, especially important for those who may wish to continue growing plants as a hobby or as a source of income.

These lights add a great dimension to programs by providing plant areas on wards or units where there is little light. They are also ideal for clients who cannot attend the greenhouse or work area. The light areas provide a haven where plants add a dimension of beauty and colour to the clients' environment.

They also set the tone for a quiet area that visitors and clients can enjoy. The proximity of these plant stands permits the clients to check their plants easily and share their knowledge and work skills with others.

Light is the energy needed by plants to produce food and other nutrients needed for growth and flowering. This process is called photosynthesis, which is the process of changing light into food. The duration of light needed for plant growth is called photoperiod. Plants require light from the violet, blue and orange part of the visible light spectrum. Red light is most important for plant growth because it promotes growth and flowering; too much red light causes plants to become tall and leggy. A full spectrum light is one rich in the colours of natural light. Lamp-watts per square foot of growing area provide an excellent basis for measuring the effectiveness of light being used. A-foot candle meter is the most reliable way to measure light amounts. A 40-watt fluorescent tube will provide light for an area of 4 feet x 6 inches (122 cm x 15.1 cm). Light intensity is lower at the ends of fluorescent tubes than in the centre. Intensity decreases with the distance from the plant. Some plants require more light than others.

## General Guide for Light Ratings Required by Plants
· Low light: 50-100 foot-candles; similar to a window facing north with trees and other obstacles blocking direct light.
· Medium Light: 200-300 foot-candles, or similar to an east or west window with no obstruction.
· Direct light: 1,200-1,500 foot-candles; similar to the sun's rays shining directly on the plant.

## Germinating Seedlings and Root Cuttings
This needs high light intensity or 1,000 foot candles. The light source should be 6-8 inches (15.1 cm-20.2 cm) above the soil or planting medium. The photoperiod is approximately 12-14 hours a day.

Vegetables and flowers for outdoor gardens can be started under the fluorescent lights, using a full spectrum light. Follow the culture guide on the package, remembering that seeds covered with vermiculite or perlite require a longer germination period.

It is also recommended that you comb or scrape the surface lightly after soaking the medium that covers the seeds, to enhance light penetration and to infuse air into the seed areas.

## Low/Medium Light Plants
Low light-intensity plants need 100-600 foot-candles for good growth. These plants will maintain their beauty for many months at 50-100 foot candles, but little growth will take place. The light source should be 12-15 inches (30.5 cm-38.2 cm) above plant tops.

## Plants
*Aglaonema* (Chinese Evergreen); *Nepthytis* (Syngonium); *Dracaena* (Corn Plant); *Phildendron* (Heart and Spade-Leafed Varieties; *Sansevieria* (Snake Plant); *Tradescantia* (Wandering Jew); Bulbs: *Narcissus, Hyacinth, Tulip, Amaryllis.*

## High Light Plants (Foliage)

The light source should be 12-15 inches (30.5 cm-38.2 cm) when four-tube fixtures are used above plant tops. The photoperiod should be approximately 14 hours a day.

## Plants

*Begonia metallica, B. rex, B. semperflorens; Cissus* rhombifolia (Grape Ivy); *Chlorophytum* (Spider Plant); *Coleus; Crassula* (Jade Plant); *Asplenium nidus* (Bird's Nest Fern); *Ficus* (Rubber Plant); *Kalanchoe; Peperomia Pilea cadieri* (Aluminum Plant); Herbs: *Allium schoenoprasum* (Chives); *Labiatae* (Mint); *Melissa officinalis* (Lemon Balm).

## Flowering Plants

These plants require 600-1,000 foot-candles and will not flower or grow at light intensities less than 100 foot candles. The photoperiod is approximately 14-16 hours daily.

*Begonia,* most flowering species; *Episcia* (Flame Violet); *Gloxinia; Impatiens; Pelargonium* (Geranium); *Saintpaulia* (African Violet).

## Culture Requirements for Plants Growing Under Artificial Light

All plant trays must be cleaned with a mild solution of water and bleach to prevent plant disease.

## Temperature

For most plants growing under lights, the temperature during the light period should be approximately 21 degrees C (70-75 degrees F.). Night time temperatures should be between 13 degrees (55 degrees F.) and 18 degrees C (65 degrees F.). Day-night temperatures are important when some plants go from a vegetative phase to a flowering or fruiting stage.

## Humidity

The ideal humidity is around 50% to 60%. Humidity is important as it reduces the amount of water lost by the plants through the leaves. During the winter months, when the humidity is often below 20%, place plants on trays filled with pebbles and water, misting foliage frequently, or use a room humidifier.

## Watering

Water plants when the lights are on. A good time period is in the morning, before temperatures start to rise. Check the soil for dryness; if it feels dry, water. Do not overwater plants or they will rot.

## Spacing

Plants should be adequately spaced to encourage disease-free plant growth and promote strong roots, stems and foliage. Do not allow plants to touch each other, as they will grow spindly, seeking light.

## Ventilation

Air circulation is important in preventing disease. Ventilation promotes the availability of carbon dioxide, necessary for photosynthesis, and oxygen, necessary for respiration. A small fan will help keep the air moving around the plants. In summer periods, fresh air from a window is ideal.

**Soil**

Use equal parts sterilized soil, peatmoss, and vermiculite or perlite. You can also use a soilless mix.

**Fertilizer**

Fertilize plants as to their requirements. (See *General Plant Care*). To prevent burning, water plants first before fertilizing. ❧

# CHAPTER

# *15*

# *Adapting Special Tools*

For some clients, gardening can be a painful, if not impossible, activity. For these individuals, the environment is a major aspect of achieving success. People who have a physical disability, or lack the essential strength to do certain garden chores, need their environment or tool to be adapted, to allow the successful performance of horticultural skills to occur. Adapting the tool or environment is the obvious and least costly approach, but for severe disabilties, special tools are available.

General garden tools, such as cultivators, hoes or rakes, should have short, sturdy handles, to ease working in a raised bed area where gardening can now be done from a sitting or standing position. (See ***Raised Bed Gardening***). This gives the client a range of motion, which is provided through the sitting or standing position. For arthritic hands, mold a sponge around the handle and secure it with carpet tape. Velcro strips or leather straps can be attached to the tops of the handles and then fastened around the forearm for added strength and ease of manoeuvring.

Long-handled tools can be adapted with a hand grip and straps so that the forearm can be padded and the tool used with one hand. Large metal trowels may be too heavy and cold to grasp, so use strong plastic trowels that are lightweight and effortless to handle. Some clients may find large soup spoons easier to dig with, especially when performing horticultural projects that require good motor skills, such as the control of the movement of soil in the planting of a terrarium. Garden trowels can also be adapted for long-handled use. The handle can be removed from the trowel and a sharpened broom handle inserted and fixed in place with a wood screw. The client can now plant from a sitting or standing positing without bending. This procedure can be done with most small hand tools, when the handle can be removed and substituted with an extension.

A piece of plastic tubing, approximately 1 inch (2.5 cm) in diameter, can be used to sow small seeds. Simply use the long-handled trowel to make the furrow, and then drop the seeds down the tube, at intervals, for the right amount of spacing.

For fine seeds, purchase or make your own seed tapes, by placing seeds on a long strip of tape at the proper distance for growing. (Check package for growing instructions). Lay the seed strip in the proper depth of earth, and cover with soil. Fine seeds can also be mixed with sharp sand for ease of handling and planting. This allows people who have problems with vision and tactile sensations, to feel the sand mixed with the seed. It also enables the client to determine where the seeds have been planted.

When using scissors, snips or small shears, a spring action tool is the best implement with which to work. This provides the client with a tool where the blades are always open and ready to cut. It is easy to use and helps strengthen weakened hand muscles. To elongate these tools, simply tape long pieces of dowling to the handles. This allows for the tool to be used with both hands, to trim or cut hard-to-reach places. A handy tool called the flower gatherer is also available. Similar to a pair of scissors, this tool can be used with either hand, and the razor sharp blades cut, clean, hold and strip the clippings. (See **Resources**).

When using watering cans, use light weight, plastic containers that have small openings. Determine the size of the can by the client's capabilities. Build a client's strength by using different sized containers. The diameter of the spout determines the rate of water flow. For clients who have severe arthritis and physical limitations, use small ketchup or mustard squeeze bottles, for easy grip and direct watering for smaller projects.

**Other Horticultural Aids**
I have found the following aids useful: spongy rubber knee pads that are comfortable and contoured to fit over the knee; straps fit snugly to keep the pads securely in place allowing clients to work closer to the ground without injury or pain. Use cotton garden gloves for light chores and special, texturized, rubber gloves when working with thorny, or rough-surfaced plants, to help prevent injury to the hands or body.

When choosing a wheelbarrow, select a cart that is stable, light, manoeuverable and does not tip easily. Larger wheelbarrows should have pneumatic tires to provide a smooth ride over rough surfaces. They should also be equipped with a "dump" front door, for easy unloading and to prevent arm and back strain. For smaller garden areas, use a wheelbarrow that has a low centre of gravity for transporting tools and garden supplies.

## Building a Pot-Lifter

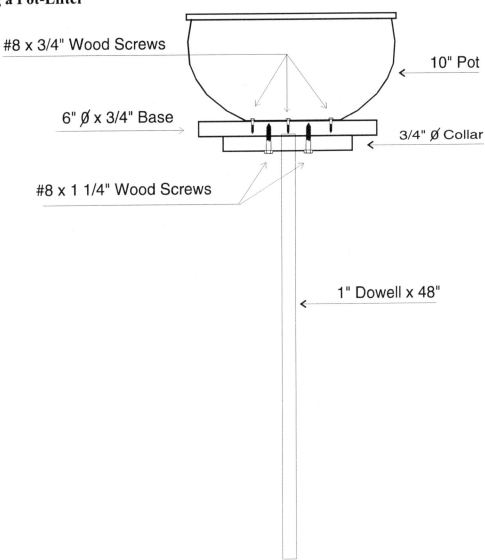

#8 x 3/4" Wood Screws

10" Pot

6" Ø x 3/4" Base

3/4" Ø Collar

#8 x 1 1/4" Wood Screws

1" Dowell x 48"

To help lift and move hanging pots, use a simple device consisting of a 4-foot long by 1-inch diamater (122 cm x 2.5cm) pole with a round plastic 10-inch (20.5 cm) hanging pot attached. It looks like a large plunger! It is made by using screws to secure the pot onto a 4-inch (10.5 cm) wooden disc attached to the pole. This allows you to easily cup this pot under and over the bottom of other pots, for ease of lifting plants up and down from a standing or sitting postion.

When working with cacti, use 5-inch (12.5 cm) plastic photo tongs for ease of removing the plant from the pot. This will allow you to work without injury from the thorns. The plastic handles are also good for gripping objects and for digging holes.

Use tongue depressors for digging, removing plants form pots, and for labelling plants. The flat smooth surface will provide the client with an easy untensil to pinch between the thumb and index finger. The flat wood surface is an ideal surface on which to print. Use a grease pencil for best results.

The most important feature for any physical disability is access either by a sloped surface or a wheel chair lift.

Tables should be raised (or lowered) to meet individual specifications. Chairs should have pads and arm rests for comfort and security. Seating clinics are now developing distinctive wheelchairs for clients with specific needs. These specialists can help the therapist determine the exact height and space allocation for tables and plant containers to be used to meet a client's needs. (See **Raised Bed Gardening**).

There are now many adaptive tools on the market for clients who have special needs. Using adaptive tools can increase clients' confidence and sense of independance. However, in order to promote this, it is important to know the tolerance levels of your clients. Work safely within the limits of their disability. Horticultural tasks should provide activities that strengthen muscles, but that do not over-exert to the extent of pain. Use the tools properly and avoid positions that promote pain and soreness. Check with the doctor for an assessment of what can and cannot be done. Rest is an important factor, guard against fatigue and take short rest breaks during work periods. ❧

# *Projects for Cognitively Impaired*

I t is imperative that you know the degree of impairment. Through your assessments and an interdisciplinary team approach, you will be able to determine the functioning level of your client. Horticultural procedures are a great way of testing concentration and retention. Whatever task or project you work with, the activity should meet your client's physical and mental capabilities. This should not be a challenge but rather a means of achieving the client's optimum level of accomplishment.

You will be able, through guided step procedures, to assess short- and long-term memory, and strengths and weaknesses. Do not go beyond a client's tolerance level. Keep your activity simple; use action words; speak clearly, and be aware of any auditory or visual impairments. If there are any physical limitations, adapt the equipment or surrounding area for optimum results. (See *Adapting Special Tools*).

**Therapeutic Objectives**
Whatever the project, the most important goal is to provide the best quality of life through an enriching experience. A sense of self-worth can be achieved through the completion of a project that is meaningful and can be used to beautify the hospital or home. This can lead to the alteration of a client's thought processes while enhancing attention span and lessening agitation.

## Testing Devices

Tasks can be interpreted and scored as a testing device to determine a client's abilities in concentration and retention. Socializing, communicating and working with the client can promote stimulation and interaction. Guided step procedures can also promote direction and eliminate confusion. Specific plant varieties will offer different textures, shapes and colours which can help to stimulate awareness and creativity.

The objective of most activities should be to have fun and be an enjoyable, nonthreatening experience. Projects can provide a sense of reality through connecting an awareness of time to a seasonal event. They should also promote a range of motion and muscle strength. The following horticultural or horticultural-related tasks have been most successful in my practice at the Homewood.

## Experiencing the Plant Environment

If clients are agitated or at a stage where there is minimal capability or response, change the environment to stimulate or alter the thought process. Walking or transporting them to an area that has plants, or even a window, offers visual stimulation. The garden, greenhouse, or solarium provide a great many sights and sensations. Emphasize points of interest that are easily identified. Action with colour may result in some sort of client response.

*Lemon Balm* (Melissa Officinalis)

## Sensory Stimulation with Herbs

This activity can be used for clients in the latter stages of dementia. Use aromatic herbs for best results. Have clients touch the leaf or rub it between their fingers, which will transfer the scent from the leaf to their hands. Allow them to "experience" this fragrance by smelling it. Repeat the name of this plant and its use. The success of this activity is not in the client remembering this information, but rather the one-to-one relationship and the caring and nurturing you provide. If a response happens, this is indeed a plus, but not the main aspect of this activity. (See *Useful Plants for Starting a Horticultural Therapy Program*).

Pull leaves from stems, using scented, nonpoisonous herbs or plants that will stimulate the senses. The product can be used in making potpourri or herb bags. Allow the client to pull or rip off pieces of leaves from the stems of selected herbs and place them on a screen to dry.

## Watering Plants with Warm Water

A small watering can is ideal, but for arthritic hands use a cylindrical, two or three inch container, such as plastic mustard or ketchup bottles. Water can be gently squeezed through the spout, individual plants watered with ease and needed exercise provided for painful joints and muscles.

## Cutting Flowers

This activity can be done anywhere, and can be done from a sitting or standing position. During the summer, if the client can go outside, balcony boxes or raised containers make this task a pleasure to do. Use spring-action secateurs if possible or medium-sized plastic scissors. Handles can be wrapped with white adhesive tape for better grip and handling.

## Pressing Flowers and Leaves

This task allows for a very passive, quieting activity useful for testing the clients' ability to identify and space different flowers and foliage onto blotter paper. This is usually done one-to-one, so clients can work at their own speed. The varieties of flowers and leaves should be easily identified through colour, shape and size. For best results, use a flower press or large wallpaper book. (See *Drying Flowers, Herbs and Greens for Pressing*).

## Preparing Potting Soil

This activity promotes a range of motion and sensory stimulation through the mixing of soil and the touching of different mediums. Give clients an apron to keep clothes clean, use sterilized soil, vermiculite, peatmoss and water to moisten. Provide three small containers filled with this material, a watering can and an empty tub for mixing. Gently guide clients' hands to each tub and get them to feel the mixture and experience the different textures. Place the three mixtures in the empty tub, water and mix. Continue this procedure until all the soil is mixed. Provide gloves or a trowel if necessary.

## Transplanting

Keep the area simple and uncluttered to prevent confusion. Use a soilless mix (cheaper, lighter and nonpoisonous, if eaten). Use contrasting colours in plant and pot choices. Tablespoons are just the right size for this task, but remember that some clients will want to put the soil into their mouths. If the client spoons the right amount of soil into the empty pot and places the root ball into this pot with the appropriate amount of soil, this will indicate good thought process and completion of a multi-stage procedure. (See *Useful Plants for Starting a Horticultural Therapy Program*).

Clients who have severe deficits should begin by holding the empty pot while you put the root ball into the pot for them. Determine if they can do this themselves by demonstrating the technique and repeating it while allowing the client to parrot this skill. (Evaluate the functioning level and strength of each hand). If they can master each step, then go to the next stage, thus maximizing the client's potential and promoting feelings of accomplishment and self worth.

## Arranging Flowers

This can be a rewarding procedure when it is made very simple. To make this an easy task for clients, select the flowers and have the vases filled with water. All of this material should be placed on a contrasting surface so that the flowers and vases are easily seen and identified. Regressed clients who can only understand a one or two-step procedure will benefit from this. Action words, such as "put the flower in the vase," removes the decision process and helps eliminate guessing and confusion. To make this a more complex task, allow clients to choose the flowers and arrange them accordingly. When this task is finished the vases are placed in the clients' rooms and dining areas. This activity not only adds beauty to their environment but gives them a sense of pride and accomplishment.

## Forcing Bulbs

This activity is usually done in the fall when Holland bulbs are available. I use pre-cooled hyacinth and daffodil bulbs, and for large, spectacular blooms, amaryllis bulbs are a must for all programs.

For best results, this project is done one-to-one. Start off by showing large colourful pictures of the plant in bloom. Red and blue are seen more easily. Most nurseries and garden centres can supply you with these. Use them, they will help enhance the project and stimulate the client.

For hyacinths and daffodils, use a 6-8 inch (15 to 20 cm) pan. Place a large soup spoon into the client's hand, gently guide this hand into a tub of soil, and begin to fill the pan half-full. When you have completed this stage, show the client how to press the bulbs into the pan (use as many bulbs as you want) and continue with the initial procedure (spooning soil on top of bulbs), but leave the tips of the bulbs showing. Water plants thoroughly, and place them in a cool room for approximately 8 to 10 weeks. Water with 20-20-20 fertilizer, when pans dry out. Bring out in the early winter months and water when dry. You will have a lovely spring-blooming plant.

When planting the amaryllis bulb, use a 6-inch (15 cm) standard pot. The method for planting this bulb is a little different. The bulb needs to sit on top of the soil, with the roots completely covered. Decide beforehand which technique you wish to use with the client, having them hold onto the bulb or spooning soil around it. To plant the amaryllis, hold the bulb in the middle of the pot with the roots facing down into it. Spoon the soil around the bulb so that it gradually fills up the pot and covering the roots so that the bulb eventually rests on top of the soil. Tamp down soil around the bulb, so it is firmly planted and does not move. Be sure to leave a 1/2 (1.25 cm) space from the top for watering. Keep this plant in a bright environment and water only when it dries out. It will produce a long stem with beautiful, large blooms.

## Washing Pots

This activity is one that has to be done constantly. It is a good activity for those clients who can benefit from a skill that will link them to the past. I have one client who enjoys this task and knows it is a job that is very necessary in the realm of growing plants. I use warm water with Sunlight soap for washing and a warm water rinse with vinegar. Pots are left to air dry and then the client gets to demonstrate their ability to store them away into the correct bins, by size. Provide rubber gloves and a chair that is comfortable for the client to sit on. The duration of this activity should be no longer than 30 minutes. You will find that some clients' skills will develop immediately, whereas others will need to break this down into stages. ❧

# CHAPTER

## *17*

# *Year-Round Calendar of Activities*

Projects are an important adjunct to therapy programs. They complement your work with clients by adding dimension and variety. All the activities described coincide with a season or event. If you are innovative and have exciting material, then you can both inspire your clients and sell your projects to help fund your program.

Most seasonal projects should be organized at least three months ahead of time to get the best quality and choice of materials. For example, when I am preparing for the fall season, I have already dried most of my material and collected grapevines and other base materials. Some materials can be collected and stored for future use such as dried flowers and cones. All of these projects require good organization, which means having all materials available and ready to use. When buying commercial goods be aware of the best buy and choose wisely to cut costs, i.e., terrarium containers, glass, clay and plastic containers and floral supplies. Never buy supplies at retail cost. Contact wholesale suppliers and let them know how they can help you. Always be on the lookout for nature's bounty and take advantage of the many free plant materials available.

I also attend gift shows during the summer months to find out about the latest design techniques and materials, such as ribbons and dried flowers. This helps keep your program current and abreast of all new styles and design materials.

If your budget is restricted, approach your place of employement with your plan of action, or contact service clubs and agencies who may be able to help you with finances.

In a group setting, divide the chores to build a sense of sharing and camaraderie. Single projects will be designed with respect to the individual's choice, but group projects require interaction between clients to promote unity and cohesiveness.

The following chapter provides a year-round, month-by-month calendar of activities and projects to help you organize your days. The next chapter gives you specifics on how these projects are done. All projects are broken into categories to assist you in preparation and completion of the project.

## *Month-by-Month Horticultural Tasks*

This section will deal with a month-by-month calendar that is divided into horticultural tasks (or tasks related to the care, growing and harvesting of plant material) and horticulturally related activities (crafts activities using plant material). This will complement your program, while at the same time providing the substance of what you will use in that program. (See *Projects*).

Here at the Homewood we are fortunate enough not only to have a greenhouse, but 47 acres of property. As you will see, our program is largely self-sustaining, since we grow much of what we use. If you are working from a solarium or using windows or grow lights, you will not have quite the flexibility we have. If so, check your locality for conservation areas and hiking trails for nature and ecology studies and as a source of natural dried materials, cones, etc. If you are using a conservation area, be sure to check with the naturalists about which material you may take away.

None of these activities is busy work! This is a program that has been developed to help clients achieve better mental health and a healthier lifestyle through a more productive and pleasurable use of leisure time.

### JANUARY

After all the activity and excitement of Christmas, January can often be a psychological let down. Now is the time to continue with a variety of activities to keep spirits up.

Horticultural Tasks: Plant shamrock seeds for St. Patrick's Day. Begin forcing flowering shrubs. (See *Forcing Flowering Shrubs*).

The following activity is a great vehicle for sensory stimulation with older adult clients. Transplant scented geraniums that were repotted in the fall.

Train pots of ivy around wire forms to create a topiary. This activity teaches pruning techniques and also provides a unique item for spring sales.

Pots of bulbs should be brought out of the cold rooms for winter bloom. These bulbs will provide colour, fragrance and the anticipation of spring. (See *Projects*).

Maintain proper culture conditions for plants in the greenhouse, under grow lights and other plant areas. During the winter months, plants need constant vigilance against insects and disease.

Horticulturally Related Projects: Design greeting or thank you cards using pressed flowers and inscribe them with calligraphy. (See *Projects*). This activity motivates clients to express thanks to those who gave them gifts, while getting them to acknowledge responsibilities and relationships outside the therapeutic environment.

Winter walks should be undertaken by clients who are physically fit and able to experience nature. This activity helps broaden and familiarize their experience with the environment, while getting them out-of-doors. Talk about bud size, to demonstrate the difference between leaves and flowers; the direction of the sun which can help determine the time of day; identify different trees by the bark; note winter birds and their feeding habits; view the winter habitat in general.

Indoors, sun catchers can be made with glass frames and dried flowers. These can be placed in clients' rooms to catch sunlight and decorate their living space.

Ordering and organizing seeds is a quieting activity that motivates clients to choose plant material for the coming season. This encourages clients to take responsibility and ownership in determining the plant material they would like to grow.

**February**
This month celebrates Valentine's Day.

Horticultural Tasks: Continue to force branches.
February is the month to start planting seeds for spring. Plant begonias, geraniums, statice, larkspur and strawflowers. Seed planting requires fine eye-hand coordination, so select those clients who can handle this task. Combination plantings can be completed with a florist pick or bow added to commemorate Valentine's Day.

Horticulturally Related Projects: Stationery can be designed with dried flowers and inscribed with calligraphy saying "Happy Valentine's Day." (See *Projects*). Small wooden hearts can also be designed with statice and other drieds for an attractive, hanging ornament.

Small bags of flowered fabric can be filled with potpourri mixtures of lavender and rose and decorated with a ribbon and small flower. (See *Projects*). This project is an excellent money-maker and can be designed for many different occasions.

Small tins and wicker containers are ideal for holding potpourri. Fill them with potpourri and decorate the lids by gluing on a small corsage.

Heart-shaped, grapevine wreaths can also be designed with drieds and an attractive bow. (See *Projects*).

A good craft sale item is almond bark made with toasted almonds mixed with chocolate. Bag it in small plastic bags. This helps generate a good source of income for the horticultural therapy program. We decorate the bags with a ribbon and attach a gold or red heart seal.

**March**
This month celebrates St. Patrick's Day.

Horticultural Tasks: Continue to force branches. As you get closer to spring, you will find that the branches force more quickly.

Pots of shamrocks are now ready to be wrapped in foil and decorated with a pick. You can use baby's tears if you do not have shamrocks.

Vegetable seeds to be planted now are cabbage, head lettuce, peppers, tomatoes and eggplant. Plant most flowering annuals for bedding plants. (See *Useful Plants for Starting a Horticultural Therapy Program*).

Contact funeral homes for a supply of fresh flowers left over from funerals. These can be used in floral design work and potpourri.

Propagate plants for future use. (See *Plant Propagation*). Continue to monitor your plants and protect tiny seedlings from the sun's strengthening rays.

Plant-up cacti dishes. Cacti tend to bloom in the early spring. Most varieties are compatible and make an attractive dish garden or can be planted singly in an attractive cup. (See *Combination Plantings*).

Horticulturally Related Projects: Continue the nature walks. Notice the subtle changes from winter to spring. Spring's arrival can be monitored and enjoyed no matter how deep the snow. Bark on dogwood and willow turns bright red and yellow, plumage on birds becomes more pronounced and the sun's rays are warmer.

Because the holiday this month is St. Patrick's Day, stationery designed with dried flowers can be inscribed with "Happy St. Patrick's Day."

**April**

Easter usually falls in April and this leads to many activities.

Horticultural Tasks: Continue to plant seeds indoors, such as: tomato, pepper, egg plant, celery, broccoli and cabbage. Outdoors, plant beets, carrots, kohlrabi, leaf lettuce, leeks, parsley, peas, radish, onions and spinach.

Harden-off annual plants by bringing them outside. Protect them from direct sun and return them indoors before nightfall.

Now is the time to get beds prepared for planting. Once the snow has left and the ground can be worked up, prepare beds by digging in organic fertilizer and planting only hardy plants such as root and salad crops. (See *Raised Bed Gardening*). Maintain indoor plants with proper culture.

Horticulturally Related Projects: Plant-up eggshells with a small, annual flowering plant such as begonia or impatiens. These can be placed in an egg cup with Easter grass and displayed as an Easter centrepiece. Plant outside in May.

Design straw or wicker hats for Easter with a bow, silk flowers and drieds. This can be attached to a client's door and makes a great conversational piece.

Grapevine baskets designed with drieds are also a popular sale item. You can also design grapevine wreaths with Easter colours.

Easter is also a time to have an open house and sale of potted plants, such as hydrangeas, African violets and geraniums, plus crafts and potpourri. Such an event can attract large turnouts, especially if well advertised.

Create combination plantings decorated with an Easter pick for an ideal centre piece. Easter stationery can be made using drieds and calligraphy.

**May**

The special occasions in May are Mother's Day and Victoria Day (Canada) and Memorial Day (USA).

Horticultural Tasks: After the 24th of May, it is usually safe to plant most flowers and vegetables out-of-doors. Indoors, sow melon and cucumber seeds. Most vegetable and flower seeds can now be sown out-of-doors.

Flower beds are now ready to be planted. (See *Useful Plants for Starting a Horticultural Therapy Program*). Landscaping techniques are taught to our substance abuse clients to foster new skills and develop positive use of leisure time You may wish to initiate a similar program.

Fertilizing plants should be done on a regular basis, beginning now and continuing throughout the summer, especially for plants growing in soilless mixes. (See *General Plant Care*).

You can begin to harvest early crops such as chives, mints and salad greens during this late May period.

Horticulturally Related Projects: For Mother's Day, obtain tea cups and plant them with miniature violets, then insert a pick displaying an appropriate greeting. Fresh flower designs and corsages can also be done for this occasion.

For Victoria Day or Memorial Day, design flowers or combination plantings and insert a small flag to signify the day. Wildflowers are in bloom in May. Gather and press them between blotter paper in presses for later use. Remember to harvest only those wildflowers that are not endangered. Also, cut branches of apple, cherry and lilac for display throughout your facility. This will help clients to relate to the time of year and the event.

Nature walks are particularly wonderful at this time of year. There is a profusion of wild flowers and the return of the birds to watch for.

May is when we have our grand sale, because by this time we have grown all our bedding plants. We use this as an opportunity to generate more income for the program. You may wish to do something similar.

Make a floral paper weight. Design a small rock by gluing on a small piece of oasis and inserting greens and dried flowers. Finish off by attaching a small mushroom bird.

It is now time to begin readying the outdoor gardens. Plant-out annuals, and cultivate and prepare beds for summer.

This is the month we have our annual spring sale. Posters and advertisements are placed throughout the facility and in the local papers. This helps generate interest and promotes the horticultural therapy program. Clients, volunteers and other staff should be organized to assist in such a venture. By selling what is produced, clients can see the results of their efforts, which can promote a positive outlook and build self-esteem.

### June

The special occasion in June is Father's Day. Clients should be encouraged to get out-of-doors regularly from now until the fall. Participating in outdoor activities promotes general health through physical fitness, fresh air and sunshine.

Horticultural Tasks: Plant melons and cucumbers out-of-doors. Make a second sowing of beans, lettuce and green onions. Maintain vegetable and herb gardens, including raised beds, flower boxes and containers.

Begin harvesting strawberries and salad crops.

Individual beds can be assigned to clients in the eating disorders program to help foster proper nutrition and a sense of independence which can be generated by caring for their own plot.

Flowers can be harvested and dried for use in future craft products. Herbs are also harvested for projects.

The garden area should be mulched to maintain moisture and control weeds.

Horticulturally Related Projects: Cut stems of perennials, such as delphinium, and peony and hang to dry.

Design a driftwood planting for Father's Day. This wonderful project can be done in a group setting. It can promote a feeling of being at one with nature, through its use of natural plants and materials. (See *Projects*).

## July
Horticultural Tasks: Gardening sessions should be done in the morning to take advantage of the cooler temperatures. Our gazebo area provides an excellent shade area in which to work on various projects, such as wiring strawflowers and tying up bunches of statice and larkspur for drying. We also press individual flowers and dry them for future projects.

Harvest cherries in July and cut and dry herbs. Also, harvest wild grapevines, make wreaths and hang them to dry.

In the greenhouse, propagate succulents as well as tropicals. (See *Plant Propagation*).

Classes can be held on shrub identification and propagation. Continue maintenance of garden areas including, watering fertilizing, spraying and harvesting.

This is a good time for field trips to botanical gardens and other greenhouses.

## August
Horticultural Tasks: Flowers, such as statice, larkspur and strawflower have reached their peak by this time at the Homewood, so most of the flowers are removed now and hung to dry. You should also continue to dry perennials such as roses, coneflower, salvia, sea lavender and goldenrod.

Horticulturally Related Projects: Because August is often a rainy month in our location, it is a good time to do terrarium designs. (See *Projects*). During the afternoon periods, large aquarium tanks and rose bowls are planted. Also, we harvest more grapevines and make them into wreaths, which are hung to dry for use in later projects.

Now is the time to order fall bulbs and soilless mixes.

**September**
This is my favourite month. I love the fall months when things start to cool down.

Horticultural Tasks: The garden should be cleaned up, the last of the tomatoes harvested and any root crops such as carrots and beets dug. All stakes and markers from the vegetable garden should be removed. All leaves and plant material from the garden should be put into the mulch pile.

Geraniums, herbs and other plants brought in before frost should be potted-up and thoroughly sprayed.

Horticulturally Related Projects: This is the month to collect and press fall leaves. Collect cones, chestnuts and acorns for fall and Christmas projects.

Nature walks during September should note the change of seasons. The juncture that is forming on the branches between a leaf and node; bird migration; seed formation; and animal behaviour, such as squirrels harvesting food.

Fall designs, such as wreaths, centre pieces and swags, can be made from grapevines, Indian corn, dried flowers and herbs.

To get the best selection and price, order all Christmas supplies now.

**October**
The special events this month are Thanksgiving (Canada), Arbour Day (USA) and Hallowe'en.

Horticultural Tasks: Out-of-doors, prepare flower beds and plant bulbs for spring bloom, such as hyacinths, daffodils, tulips and crocus. Mulch plants such as strawberries, roses and newly planted perennials. Fruit trees should be protected by wrapping the trunk with plastic collars and shrubs wrapped in burlap for winter protection. All shrubs should be given a good soaking before cold temperatures set in. Remove soil from A-frames and portable, raised bed containers and store them for the winter.

Indoors, plant the same bulbs and store in a cold room, or in a cool dark space, for forcing.

Horticulturally Related Projects: Remove all the garden hoses from outside taps and store for the winter. Clean and oil garden tools and store.

Bird feeders should be filled now to begin attracting birds.

Stationery can be designed for Thanksgiving and pumpkins carved for Hallowe'en. Also, do arrangements of gourds, pumpkins, squash and Indian corn for display throughout your facility. Arrangements of dried flowers can be placed on dining room tables.

Herbs and small tropical plants should be placed under the grow lights.

**November**

Remembrance Day (Canada) and Veteran's Day and Thanksgiving (USA) are the holidays observed this month.

Horticultural Tasks: Propagate such plants as wandering Jew, spider plants, begonias, German and English Ivy using Rocket Packs. (See *Plant Propagation*). Also, plant cactus gardens. Water the pans of fall bulbs stored in the cold room.

Horticulturally Related Projects: As the holidays are very important to older adult clients, the following activities can be done to commemorate these days. Using poppies donated by the Canadian Legion, we decorate straw wreaths. We fill vases with poppies taped onto a wire stem with green leaves and place these in client dining rooms. War memorabilia are loaned by clients and used as a focus for our display window.

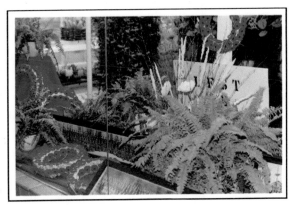

Collected nuts should be drilled for Christmas projects and you should begin making cone wreaths and centre-pieces.

Potpourri should be made and stored for Christmas projects as well.

**December**

This festive season provides an abundance of wonderful activities.

Horticultural Tasks: Get outside and cut a variety of greens, for Christmas centrepieces. Plant-up combination plantings using tropical plants, and complement with a Christmas florist pick. (See *Combination Plantings*).

Shamrock seeds should be planted for March and hydrangeas should be forced for Easter.

My grandmother used to make this charming arrangement for an old, European Christmas centrepiece. Plant a shallow container with oats and place a red pillar candle in the centre.

Prune hanging plants and use the cuttings for propagation.

Horticulturally Related Projects: You can make all of the following: pine cone designs, miniature glass ball terrariums, grapevine designs, natural bark designs, Christmas stationery, Christmas corsages, fresh flower designs, using evergreens and cones and potpourri. (See *Projects).*

Have a Christmas bazaar or sale. This is the perfect time to bring out everything you've made during the year. Don't forget the vinegars, dried flowers and herbs. Use wicker baskets, ceramic pots and foil to compliment your plant sale.

Also, do an abundance of pine cone designs. Pine cones on driftwood, wreaths, boards and centre-pieces. In short, cones can be placed on almost every surface for Christmas decoration!

**Augmenting the Program**

To augment horticultural therapy programs, provide a variety of audio visual materials on a range of horticultural topics. Set up field trips to botanical or public gardens, universities, and horticultural industry companies; also special events like maple syrup-making, flower festivals, fall leaf tours and fairs can be scheduled.

Seed companies usually have their own unique gardens with new varieties of plants.

Libraries are a great resource for researching and broadening the perspective of your program.

Invite guest speakers from educational institutions, horticultural clubs, and plant and craft enthusiasts.

Remember to keep you program progressive and innovative, to stimulate your clients, staff and volunteers.

*Please Note*: Many seed catalogues indicate hardiness zones. If you are not sure what your zone is, check with a local nursery or in Ontario, contact the county offices of the Ministry of Agriculture and Food. Readers in other provinces and countries should do likewise. United States readers should consult with their agricultural extension agents. ❧

CHAPTER

# *18*

# *Projects*

The following projects and activities can be broken down into many stages to suit the client's capabilities, or they can be made more challenging to provide some degree of difficulty for problem-solving. Projects will be listed for the populations they are most suited to, with the following codes: Alcohol Abuse (AL), Drug Addiction (D), Schizophrenia (Scz), Affective Disorders (AD), Anorexia Nervosa (AN), Cognitive Impairment (CI). (See ***Populations and Diagnostic Categories***).

Projects listed are designed to help the therapist bring creativity and imagination to the Horticultural Therapy Program. These activities provide a variety of tasks to accent the different occasions throughout the year.

There are many styles and techniques in performing these skills. I have found that all these projects will provide a sound basis to accent your program.

Projects listed are guides to stimulate the client into developing further interest in the realm of horticulturally-related activities.

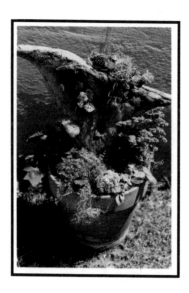

## *Driftwood Plantings*

Purpose:  To create a natural looking planting for growing indoors.

Population:  (AL), (D), (Scz), (AD), (AN).

Background:  This project is the result of a fishing and camping trip in Northern Ontario.  The beauty of the lakes and natural terrain were my inspiration for this activity.  I saw driftwood  from fallen trees lodged in craggy shore lines, with mosses, ferns and other plant life growing abundantly on its surface. A closer look revealed other plant life and even small birds nesting in higher parts of the bleached wood.  I knew I could duplicate this natural look by creating my own miniature landscape.  I also found many other interesting treasures to collect, such as sun bleached driftwood, colourful pebbles, shells and reindeer and ground moss.

Fallen trees can provide unusual pieces of bark and interesting chunks of white and yellow fungus.  For the keen eye, small uninhabited bird nests and dried weeds can give an earthy look to a design. However, I never remove rare plants and I only use those plants that are prolific.  This ensures that the balance of nature is maintained and the landscape left for others to enjoy.  The material for this project is usually collected with groups on guided nature walks and I always remind clients to respect and care for the natural environment, so that others can experience and appreciate it.  When this project is completed, you will have captured the memory of where and when you collected this material.  I can still hear the sound of loons on the lakes and smell the sweet odour of pine and cedar during my early morning hikes.

Collecting these materials and experiencing the outdoors is a great activity by itself.  Be sure clients are sufficiently fit to handle such a walk and wear protective clothing and proper hiking boots.  Take along insect repellant and small plastic bags for collecting.  For clipping dried weeds, a pair of secateurs is a must.

### Materials

Driftwood:  Collect pieces from 12-36 inches (30-76 cm).  The size of the driftwood determines the size of the planting.  Make sure it is fairly clean and insect-free.  Place driftwood into a full sun area and let it dry out.  Brush off any soil or debris and spray the wood with a solution of two tablespoons of bleach to a pint of water (30 ml bleach to 473 ml water).

Container:  A 12-15 inch (30.5-38.2 cm) clay pot is ideal.  The pot should be able to hold the driftwood in place and allow for the potting medium to be placed around it.  Soak the pot for an hour before planting to prevent soil from drying out.

Gravel or Small Stones: Use this rock material in the bottom of the pot, to stabilize the driftwood.

Soil Mixture: Use equal parts of peatmoss, sterilized soil and perlite.

Plants: Small tropical and wayside plants can be used to simulate a natural look. Use a variety of plant sizes, including pendulous and upright varieties.

Tropicals: *Pilea* (Aluminum Plant), *Pteris species* (Pteris Fern), *Nephrolepis veronica carigii* (Dwarf Boston Fern), *Araucaria heterophylla* (Norfolk Island Pine), *Pilea depressa* (Creeping Jenny), *Cissus rhombifolia* (Grape Ivy), *Fittonia argyroneura nana* (Nerve Plant), *Helixine soleirolii* (Baby's Tears), *Davallia canariensis* (Rabbit's Foot Fern).

Wayside Plants: Young's red cedar, common cedar, ebony spleenwort, lichen, cladonia, reindeer and ground moss and fungi growing on decayed wood.

Birds: Small flocked or mushroom bird, spanish moss or bird's nest.

Glue Gun: May be used to glue the nest and bird or fungus onto the wood, if there is no cavity in the wood

## Procedure

Step 1: Place clean driftwood into the clay container with branches or pieces of wood standing upwards to give an interesting look.

Step 2: Fill the container one-third full with gravel or small stones.

Step 3: Fill the remainder of the container with soil mixture to within one or two inches of the rim. Press down firmly to make sure the driftwood holds firmly in place.

Step 4: Design your planting to complement the shape of the wood, then begin arranging plants around the driftwood. Place small ferns in any crevices. Taller plants can be planted alongside the wood for balance. For interest, create small hills or depressions with soil. Do not over-plant; simple can be elegant! To remove plants from pots, gently turn the pot upside down and tap on its rim and remove the plant careuflly. This is an effective technique for removing most plants from pots.

Step 5: Use your collection of materials to enhance the planting and to create a rugged scene. Moss can be placed into corners of the wood or on soil areas. Use the glue gun to attach moss to the wood. Stones and coloured gravel can be placed into pockets of the wood and fanned out into soil areas. Fungus pieces and bird's nest or Spanish moss can be hot-glued onto the wood or pushed into crevices of the wood. Mushrooms or a flocked bird can be placed into the nest or hot-glued onto the wood.

## Care of the Driftwood Planting

Place this planter in an eastern exposure or in filtered afternoon sun. Moisten the soil well with room temperature water. Fertilize once per month from April to September with 20-20-20 fertilizer, or a balanced natural fertilizer such as fish emulsion. Prune occasionally to keep plants in shape and prevent woody growth. Spray occasionally with Safer's soap to prevent insect infestation. Enjoy!

## Therapeutic Application

For those individuals who are physically able, some of these materials can be collected on a guided nature walk. For others, this project is an interesting design piece that can be done in a group or individually. Although this planting can be done by a variety of clients, it has more of a masculine appeal due to the strength and rugged look of the driftwood and clay pot.

## Terraced Terrariums

Purpose:  To design a multi-level terrarium.

Population:  (AL), (D), (Scz), (AD), (AN), (CI).

Background:  This idea came from a desire to develop a project that would be cheaper and more distinctive than commercially bought terrariums, contribute beauty to the hospital environment and provide clients with instant gratification.

### Materials

Containers:  Clear glass containers, such as fish bowls or aquarium tanks, rose bowls, pickle jars, demijohns or small fruit juice bottles.  Wash containers and rinse in a solution of one cup vinegar to one gallon warm water.

Soil Mixture:  Equal parts of sterilized soil, peatmoss and perlite or vermiculite.  A soilless mixture can also be used.  Perlite will provide aesthetics and drainage.  The amount of this growing medium you use is determined by the size of your container.

Wood or Bark:  This is used to create a plateau or division.  This can also be done without the bark by firming the soil into steps.

Plants:  The plants you use must be able to tolerate high humidity, provide colour, texture and be slow growing.  Always choose healthy plants that are free of insects and do not have broken or bruised leaves.  Select plants with different heights and sizes.

Tall Plants:  *Maranta tri colour* (Herringbone Plant), *Neanthe bella* (Dwarf Palm), *Peperomia caperate* (Dwarf Peperomia), *Pilea cadierei* (Watermelon Plant).

Medium and Pendulous Plants:  *Saxifraga sarmentosa* (Strawberry Begonia), *Hedera helix* (English Ivy), *Fittonia argyroneura nana* (Nerve Plant), *Cryptanthus* (Earth Star), *Pilea mollis* (Moon Valley Pilea), *Pilea microphylla muscosa* (Artillery Plant).

Accents:  Pebbles, shells, coloured aquarium gravel, driftwood, reindeer moss and small branches.

### Procedure

Step 1:  Make sure the container is clean, see above cleaning method.  If container has seams, turn the lines to the side so your design can be seen clearly without seams distorting your view.

Step 2:  Begin by spooning one inch of perlite onto the bottom of the container, for drainage.

Step 3:  Spoon or shovel the soil mixture into the container so that it forms a slope effect.  Press bark into the middle of soil and shape it into two plateaus, top and bottom. These plateaus should look like two steps. (The same technique can be done in an aquarium tank, where small hills and depressions can be made without the use of the wood.) You can make more divisions or steps according to the size of your container.

Step 4: Choose your plants, and arrange them beside the container as you plan your design. Be sure to use a good variety of colours and shapes, so that your finished effect has dimension and character. Gently tap plants out of their pots; remove most of the soil from the roots; dig a hole, and plant into the desired location. Tall plants should go to the back of the container, while pendulous varieties can cascade over the bark area. Plant small specimens to the front. Be creative, but avoid over-planting, as plants fill in fast. If plants appear too large or bushy, prune back some of the tips or safely divide plants.

Step 5: After plants have been tamped into place, use collected materials for creating a natural scene. Aquarium gravel, pebbles and shells can be displayed in the corners of the terrarium. Wood chips can form paths, while moss placed throughout can give a textured look to complement the plant and draw out the interesting shapes and veins of the leaves.

Step 6: Water plants by gently pouring room-temperature water down your hand. Use a small piece of wood to extend water flow. Do not over-water; wipe off excess moisture with a paper towel when completed.

**Care of the Terrarium**

Place the terrarium in indirect light; direct sun is too hot. Water when the soil appears dry. Do not fertilize, as this will speed up the growth of the plants and cause them to outgrow the container in a short period of time. If insects appear on the plants, use a brush dipped in alcohol and apply directly to the affected area.

These projects are a great way of using pickle jars and other interesting glass containers. They make wonderful, inexpensive additions to any environment and are easy to care for. Terrariums are ideal for propagating and starting small plants, as they provide humidity and moisture. The best choice of container to use with clients who have visual or physical impairment is an aquarium, because of its size and opening. Prune occasionally to maintain desired shapes. Enjoy!

## Forcing Bulbs

Purpose: To force bulbs for winter bloom indoors.
Population: (AL), (D), (Scz), (AD), (AN), (CI).
Background: Bulbs must be planted in September and October for early varieties to bloom during Christmas time. Forcing bulbs for the purpose of having spring blooms in the winter months always brings a great deal of joy and interest. The colour and fragrance can stimulate the senses and may alter depression. The flowering plants are ideal for special occasions such as Valentine's Day, St. Patrick's Day and Easter.

### Materials

Plants: Purchase pre-cooled bulbs such as tulips, daffodils, hyacinths, crocus, freesia and amaryllis.
Growing Medium: Equal parts of sterilized soil, peatmoss and perlite. You can also use a soilless mix.
Drainage Material: Clay chips or pebbles.
Containers: 6-8 inch (15-20 cm) clay or plastic bulb pans; size is determined by the number of bulbs you wish to plant.

### Procedure

Step 1: Soak clay pots in water for one hour before planting.
Step 2: Cover drainage holes with one half inch (7 cm) of gravel or cover holes with clay chips if using a soil mixture.
Step 3: Fill container with soil mixture within two inches (5 cm) of the bottom of the bulb.
Step 4: Press bulbs into the soil and fill medium around them, to within one inch below the container's rim. Firm down soil to stabilize bulbs. The number of bulbs you plant is determined by the size of the container. Plant tulips with the flat side of the bulb on the outside of the container so that the leaves will develop over the rim; the tips of bulbs should show through the soil
Step 5: Submerge the container in water to the rim; the bulbs will not be disturbed through bottom watering.
Step 6: Place a label in each pot showing the variety and date of planting.
Step 7: Place the pan of bulbs in a cold room or frost-free location, such as a cellar or garage, so that the temperature is about 40-45 degrees F. (3-10 degrees C.).
Step 8: During the forcing period, the bulb pans must be kept in a dark place. Water only when soil appears dry. Root development will vary according to the kind of bulb and blooming period.

Depending on the variety, it may take from 8-15 weeks. The nursery or supplier can give you a guide on the approximate period for bloom.

Step 9: Check for root and shoot development. If roots are growing out from the drainage holes and the shoots are one to one and a half inches tall, move plants indoors. Place in a cool location and keep shaded for approximately one week, gradually exposing the bulbs to increased temperature and light.

Step 10: Continue the watering procedure and fertilize with a weak solution of 20-20-20.

Step 11: Plants will bloom in approximately 4-6 weeks.

## Forcing Amaryllis

Step 1: The container should be at least two inches larger than the diameter of the bulb.

Step 2: If using a soil mixture, place drainage in the bottom.

Step 3: Hold the bulb with one hand, so that the roots of the plant are hanging down into the pot, and begin filling the pot with soil. The medium should cover the roots with the bulb resting firmly within the soil. The soil level should be within one inch of the rim of the pot, with the bulb rising out of the soil.

Step 4: Water well and let the soil dry out between watering.

Step 5: Keep the pot in a warm, shaded spot until the flower stalk is 6-8 inch (15 cm-20 cm) tall. Move the plant into an area so that the blooms can be enjoyed by all.

Step 6: After flowering, cut off the flower stalk and continue to grow the plant in a sunny window, or move it outdoors in the spring to a shady location.

## Therapeutic Application

Bulbs are easy to handle and plant since they have a definite shape and strength. Amaryllis produce large colourful blooms that can stimulate a client's involvement and interest in horticulture.

*Forsythia* (Golden Bells)

## *Forcing Flowering Branches*

Purpose: To force flowering branches into bloom during winter months.
Population: (AL), (D), (Scz), (AN).
Backgorund: During the winter months this activity helps boost clients' spirits. The vibrant yellow flowers of forsythia or the oriental look of flowering quince will add visual and aromatic appeal to any room. Snowshoeing, walking or crosscountry skiing in search of branches is a great way to enjoy exercise in the winter months.

### Materials
Use a good pair of secateurs (pruning sheers).
A large plastic bag for carrying the branches.
Elastics or twist ties to wrap around stems.
Large vases or pickle jars filled with water.
Misting bottle.

Flowering Shrubs: *Forsythia* (Golden Bells), *Chaenomeles* (Flowering Quince), *Prunus cistena* (Purple Leaf Sandcherry), *Salix discolour* (Pussy Willow), (Saucer Magnolia), *Hamamelis* (Chinese Witch Hazel).
Trees: *Prunus triloba* (Flowering Almond), *Cornus stolonifera* (Dogwood), *Malus* (Apple), *Prunus* (Cherry), Saucer Magnolia.

### Procedure
Choose a sunny day, when the temperature is above freezing; sap flow is heightened at these temperatures and promotes a better flower development. Branches should be at least one half inch (1.25 cm)

thick in order for flowers to develop properly. Young stems tend to force best from new wood. Note the difference between a leaf bud and a flower bud; flower buds are usually round and fat, while leaf nodules are thin and have a distinctive point. To maximize the quality of blooms, choose branches with many flower buds.

Step 1: Cut branches flush with the stem of the tree or bush. Pruning will promote new growth and will help to shape the plant.

Step 2: Tree and shrub branches look alike, so bundle them and put an elastic around each variety.

Step 3: After you have harvested your branches, the process for forcing them is fairly straightforward. Remove 2 inches (5 cm) of bark from the base of the stem, and cut up into it from the bottom in two places, making an "x". This will allow water absorption to occur within the stem. Another method is to pound the base of the stem until the wood is broken up.

Step 4: Place stems into vases or jars of warm water and store them in a dark room for five days.

Step 5: Change water frequently, to prevent it from becoming stagnant.

Step 6: Mist buds daily, to provide essential humidity.

Step 7: After 5 days bring branches into the daylight (cool, morning light is best), and continue misting and changing the water. In approximately 14-24 days, you will have a beautiful spring bouquet!

**Blooming Period**

Forsythia: Bright yellow blooms in approximately 21 days.

Flowering Quince: Range of pinks/reds in approximately 15 days.

Purple Leaf Sandcherry: Pink blossoms with a delicate fragrance that blooms in approximately 21 days.

Pussy Willow: Branches should not be left in the water past their prime.

Saucer Magnolia: Large white/pink blooms in approximately 24 days.

Chinese Witch Hazel: Flowers only a short time, but unique in shape and design, approximately 21 days.

Flowering Almond: Delicate pink flowers, approximately 24 days.

Dogwood: Beautiful stems that produce delicate white flowers in approximately 21 days.

Apple: Fragrant white/pink blooms in 24 days.

Cherry: Classy, elegant, delicate flower and scent; arrange in porcelain vase, 24 days to maturity.

**Therapeutic Application**

This activity encourages clients to venture outside for a guided nature tour. Activities include collecting and preparing stems and arranging stems in vases.

This project provides anticipation for early spring bloom, or delayed gratification.

Wandering Jew and Aluminum Plant

## *Plant Propagation*

Purpose: To grow and propagate tropical plants.
Population: (AL), (D), (Scz), (AD), (AN), (CI).
Background: Propagating and growing plants is the basis of most horticultural therapy programs. Propagating plants provides an excellent avenue for clients to learn about horticulture and the techniques of how to produce their own plants. This activity reduces the cost of buying plant material, and provides stock for projects and plant sales.

### Materials

Plants: I have found the following plants to be vigorous and easy to root: Coleus, *Tradescantia* (Wandering Jew), *Plectranthus neutralis* (Swedish Ivy), *Chlorophytum comosum* (Spider Plant), *Pilea microphylla* (Artillery Plant), Peperomia, *Saintpaulia* (African Violet), Impatiens and *Saxifraga sarmentosa* (Strawberry Begonia).
Containers: Small pots, flats with a clear plastic cover, or rocket packs. I use rocket packs because they are the easiest containers with which to work. They are styrofoam plant cells that allow you to plant many cuttings in one container. Clients are able to fill these effortlessly because of the shape, colour and size. These containers are also stable on the table and do not fall over.
Growing Medium: Use equal parts of vermiculite and perlite.
Tools: Small trowels or soup spoons, scissors, a knife and a watering can.

### Procedure

Step 1: Always propagate plants from healthy stock.
Step 2: Propagate plants such as Coleus, *Plectranthus neutralis* (Swedish Ivy), *Tradescantia* (Wandering Jew) and *Pilea microphylla* (Artillery Plant) by stem cuttings. Plants such as *Chlorophytum comosum* (Spider Plant) and *Saxifraga sarmentosa* (Strawberry Begonia) are propagated from runners called plantlets. African Violets, Peperomia and some Begonias are propagated by leaf cuttings.
Step 3: For plants propagated by stem cuttings, use a knife or scissors to perform the cutting. The stem should be approximately 3-4 inches (8.5-10.5 cm) long. Cut the stem on a slant below a node and cut

off all flowers and buds. Remove leaves from the lower 2-3 inches (6-8 cm) of the stem. The top leaves should be left to produce the food needed for growth. Plant the cuttings in containers filled with a rooting medium, tamp firmly, water and keep medium moist. Plants will root in approximately 2-3 weeks. Pot up in a 1-1 1/2inches (4-5 cm) container or plant trailing varieties in a 5-6 inch (12-15 cm) hanging pot.

For plants propagated from runners, cut the plantlet off the runner and insert it into the rooting medium. Keep moist; plants will form roots in approximately two to three weeks. Follow the same procedure for potting as for stem cuttings.

For plants propagated from leaf cuttings (with stems), trim the stem of the leaf to 1 inch (2.5 cm) and press the leaf onto the growing medium. Cut notches into the veins of each leaf. Plants will form in approximately 2 months. Carefully separate and plant into a 2-inch pot (5 cm).

## Growing Tips
Grow at a daytime temperature of 70 degrees F. (20 degrees C.) with a night time temperature not less than 60 F. (16 C.). Always use room temperature water, and allow plants to dry out between waterings. Keep plants away from cold drafts after they have been transplanted. Fertilize with an all purpose plant food such as 20-20-20.

## Therapeutic Application
To provide plant material for a variety of projects, propagating plants should be done throughout the year .

## *Drying Flowers and Greens*

Purpose: To dry plant material for future projects.

Population: All populations.

Background: This task provides a two-fold activity: cutting and collecting the plant material, and the preparation, pressing and storing of the finished product for future projects. This gives you an excellent vehicle for your work with clients and provides a variety of skill levels. The collection and identification of this material is done on a nature walk. However, plant material can also be grown in raised beds for easy access. The end product of collecting or growing good quality plant material is that it supplies you with resources for doing a variety of projects throughout the year. Every month has an occasion to use this material. I recommend this activity as a major project for any program.

### Materials

Tools for Collecting: Scissors, cardboard box (pop box base container used for packaging soft drinks).

Flower Press: Use an 8 1/2 x 11 inch wooden press that has four metal screws with metal washers and wing nuts.

Blotter paper: Use to remove moisture from plants.

Cardboard: Cut pieces of cardboard the same size as the blotter paper and use to separate sections.

Other: Cardboard boxes for storing dried material, paint brush for ease of removing flower heads from blotter paper and silica gel, (small packages that can be obtained from the pharmacy)  This gel aids in keeping the material from absorbing moisture).

Plants: The ideal plant materials to press are flowers that are not large, juicy, or have thickness; flat, round shapes and paper-textured flowers are ideal. Small leaves, grasses and ferns provide you with colour and proportion.

Annual Flowers:  *Alyssum sp.* (Sweet Alyssum), *Delphinium, Viola* (Pansy), *Gypsophila* (Baby's Breath), *Linum* (Flax), *Lobelia, Myosotis* (Forget-me-not), *Nigella* (Love-in-a-mist) and *Viscaria* (Blue Angel).

Perennial Flowers:  *Brunnera* (Forget-me-not), *Delphinium, Limonium* (Sea Lavender), *Phlox, Platycodon* (Balloon Flower), *Viola* (Pansy), *Vinca* (Periwinkle) and *Scilla* (Bluebell).

Flowering Shrubs:  *Calluna* (Heather), *Deutzia, Erica* (Winter Heather), *Forsythia* (Golden Bells), *Hydrangea, Kolkwitzia* (Beauty Bush), *Potentilla* (Shrubby Cinquefoil) and *Spiraea* (Bridal Wreath).

Be creative and experiment with different varieties.

Leaves, Grasses and Ferns: Choose small varieties: almost any green material will do, as long as it is thin and does not have a great deal of moisture within the plant.

## Procedure for Collecting and Cutting Materials

Step 1: Always collect material in the morning when the moisture has evaporated off the plant and sun has not wilted it.

Step 2: Cut the bloom from the plant, leaving only a short stem. The size of the flower should not be any bigger than 2 inches in circumference. Green material can be larger, because it has less water content.

Step 3: Place collected material in a cardboard box for easy carrying.

Step 4: Use material within a short period of time to prevent shrivelling.

## Procedure for Pressing and Storing

Step 1: Make sure flower heads are clean and dry before pressing.

Step 2: Cut off flower heads from stems, and remove any green. Place flower heads on the surface of the blotter paper, with either the heads down or facing upward. Blooms may also be pressed sideways for a different look. Space evenly on the blotter paper so that edges of the flowers are not touching. This prevents build-up of moisture and discolouring of flowers. When pressing leaves, ferns and grasses, cut the pieces to fit the press and then space them sufficiently apart to prevent moisture build-up.

Step 3: Once the blotter paper is filled, place another sheet of blotter paper over the material to create a "sandwich effect." Cardboard may be placed between sections of pressed flowers to promote air circulation.

Step 4: When the press is full, position the lid down over the screws and put the metal washers in place; tighten the wing nuts securely, to press all material in place.

Step 5: Affix a label on the outside of the press, with the date and material that has been pressed.

Step 6: Allow 4 weeks for material to dry completely.

Step 7: To remove flowers and other pressed material, gently lift the blotter paper off each section and remove the plant material with your fingers, or use a small paint brush if it sticks to the paper.

Step 8: Separate this material and place it into small card boxes, with a small package of silica gel.

Label the edge of each box with the name of the flower.

Step 10: Store in a warm, dry cupboard for future use.

## *Pinecone Designs*

Purpose:  To make a variety of cone designs using collected material.

Population:  These projects can be worked on by a variety of populations.

Background:  Cone projects add a great deal of dimension to horticultural therapy programs during special seasons.  For people who are cognitively impaired, it promotes time of year and helps clients stay in touch with reality.  For active clients, the collecting of this material can provide intellectual stimulus through classes on identification of trees and their life cycles.  Cone projects provide a meaningful activity to assist clients in working through their goals and objectives.  Design strategies are stimulated, and, working in a group setting promotes an appropriate outlet for interaction and sharing (feelings) with others.  Finished products can enhance self-esteem and build positive leisure skills.  Physical aspects include increased strength through walking, bending and general range of motion. Sorting the cones stimulates thought processes and involves fine, eye-hand co-ordination.

### Materials

Natural materials should be collected when they are available; when possible they should be collected throughout the year.  Always be on the lookout for any natural materials, such as weeds or seed pods.  When you attempt these projects, the essential consideration is to have all the material collected ahead of time!

Cones:  Collect various sizes and varieties, such as pine, spruce and hemlock cones.

Nuts: Collect chestnuts, acorns and other hard-shelled nuts.  Please note that nuts and other hard shell items should have holes drilled into them for ease of wiring.

Other Material:  Florist's wire (thin gauge); a good pair of wire cutters; wire frames.  (There are a variety of wire frame sizes available at most craft or florist supply shops); sahara oases, glue guns and clear lacquer spray.  To trim finished projects, use lacquered berries, ribbons, and a small decoration to compliment the season, i.e., a bird or greeting pick.  For the miniature tree, use a clay pot with a variety of drieds, such as statice and coloured baby's breath.

Styrofoam Bases:  Use cone shapes or round shapes for tree and table designs.

### Procedure for Cone Wreath

Step 1: Decide what size wreath you would like to make.  A 10-12 inch (25.5-30.5 cm) is generally the best size with which to begin.

Step 2: Place the wreath frame upside down, so that the rounded part is facing down. Begin by inserting approximately 20, 5-6 inch (12.5-15.25 cm) long spruce cones into the wreath frame. The cones should slide through the wire frame and the base of the cone should extend one inch (2.5 cm) beyond the inner wire frame, to secure it in place. Continue this procedure, pushing and turning cones into the frame until you have completely filled the frame. You may need more cones to form a solid base.

Step 3. The next step can be done in a variety of ways, but I have found this the most effective method: Begin wiring round pinecones into groups of three. Using two pieces of florist's wire, press three cones together to form a tripod. Bend each wire in half and place around the cones and twist tightly, leaving wire ends protruding from one side of the cones. With the other piece of wire, repeat this procedure so that the wire now extends from both sides of the cones. The finished effect should look like a "bow tie."

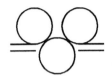

Step 4: Lie the wreath frame flat, with the rounded, wide side facing up. Place the triangle of cones on top of the wire ridge of spruce cones. Insert wires through the wreath and tie both pieces together to secure pine cones onto the frame. To give the wreath character, wire the next group of cones upside down, so that the flat part of the cone is facing up. Continue wiring all cones into place, or be creative and come up with your own design.

Step 5: Wire small cones and nuts throughout the wreath to give it a rich blend of colours and textures. Fasten wires to the back of the wreath frame, to ensure all cones and nuts stay in place.

Step 6: Turn the wreath over and twist all hanging wires tightly, then cut wire ends to 1-inch (2.5 cm). Push wire ends into the wreath to prevent any scratching surfaces.

Step 7: Spray the entire wreath with a clear, high gloss lacquer. This should be done out of doors. Allow the wreath to dry for 2 hours.

Step 8: Use rich, festive colours and textures, such as red velvet, green parchment and berries to complement the design. Arrange ribbon, lacquered berries and ornaments into place before hot-gluing. Other suggestions for wreaths with a natural look are small nests, birds and Spanish moss. For musical or animal themes, use a small brass instrument or a teddy bear, following through with matching ribbons and ornaments.

Step 9: Cover the back of the wreath. Measure the diameter of the frame, cut out a matching circle of felt in a doughnut shape and hot-glue this onto the back of the wreath.

## Procedure for Miniature Pinecone Tree

Step 1: Select a 3-inch (7.5 cm) pine cone, preferably in a round, open shape.

Step 2: Glue the pinecone onto a 1/2 inch (1.25 cm) clay pot.

Step 3: Dab glue into the crevices of the pinecone and decorate with pieces of salvia, baby's breath or small flowers.

Step 4: Tie a coordinating bow around the outer lip of the pot.

## Therapeutic Application

This project is ideal for clients with cognitive impairment, as it has limited step procedures. The finished design can be used as a centrepiece or for a name tag at a table.

## Procedure for Pinecone Tree

Step 1: Spray styrofoam cone with brown lacquer.
Step 2: Wire all small cones approximately one and a half inches in diameter (2.25-4 cm). Dip the wires in ceramic tile adhesive and push into the cone. Start at the base and work around in a circle, building on each level until you get to the top. Use small hemlock or spruce cones to fill in any gaps.
Step 3: Use small nuts or acorns to fill in any holes. This will give the tree lustre and character after it has been sprayed.
Step 4: Spray the tree with a clear, high gloss or satin finish lacquer.
Step 5: Allow the tree to dry for approximately 2 hours. Decorate with small berries or drieds.
Step 6: Finish by decorating the tree with a small bow or ornament. Cut a circular piece of felt the same size as the base of the tree, and glue the material onto the bottom of the tree to protect surfaces from wires.

## Procedure for Pinecone Centrepiece

Step 1: Cut styrofoam ball in half with a sharp knife. This will provide you with two, half spheres. The size can vary from 3-5 inches (7.5-12.5 cm) in diameter. The size of the ball determines the size and length of the candle.
Step 2: Place the flat side of the sphere down and press a candle into the middle of the rounded base.
Step 3: The candle will allow you to hold the design easily, so that you can spray the base evenly with brown lacquer.
Step 4: Begin by dipping the smallest, wired spruce cones into ceramic tile adhesive. Working in a circle, start at the bottom and work your way around until you have a solid ring. Continue to build another ring on top of each level until you get to the candle.
Step 5: Fill in any holes with small, wired nuts or cones.
Step 6: Spray the design with high gloss lacquer.
Step 7: After the design has dried, add small artificial berries, by dipping stems into the adhesive and carefully piercing them through the design into the styrofoam. Finish centrepiece by complementing it with a small bow and ornament.

## Procedure for Christmas Tree Ornament

Begin by hot-gluing a small piece of sahara oasis onto the flat base of a long cone, remembering to keep the design material in proportion to the cones. This design is done on the flat part of the cone. Use a flower pot to help hold the cone in an upright position while designing.

Step 1: Begin with the largest cone you can find, and cover the oasis on its flat end with a small piece of Spanish moss.

Step 2: Hot-glue or pierce-in three small dried leaves into the middle of the base of the oasis, with the leaves radiating down each side to give you a green base with which to begin.

Step 3: Attach a small bow into the middle of the leaves.

Step 4: Hot-glue or pierce a variety of small drieds, cones and berries around the bow area. Add a small bird for colour.

Step 5: The final stage is making a loop to hang the finished ornament. This is done by hot-gluing both ends of the desired length of ribbon into the middle of the cone.

## Therapeutic Application

Cone projects provide pleasure for most clients and add dimension to horticultural therapy programs during special seasons. The style and design of each project is determined by the rich colour and distinctive shapes of the cones. For active clients capable of doing these projects, an excellent therapeutic experience can be provided through this demonstration of their creative skills. Clients can keep projects, or they can be used for decoration of their environment, or as bazaar items. These attractive projects help to raise awareness of the horticultural therapy program. Results of the finished products can enhance self esteem and build positive leisure skills. Physical aspects include: increased strength through walking, bending and general range of motion. Sorting and wiring cones stimulates thought processes and promotes fine, eye-hand coordination.

## Table and Wall Design Using Natural Material

Purpose: To create unique designs using wood and bark.

Population: These activities can be accomplished by a variety of populations who are physically able to collect the material and participate in a creative hands-on project.

Background: This project has a two-fold purpose: collecting the material on a nature walk and creating and designing with the collected materials. Using natural materials is a great way of cutting costs and adding a native or rustic appeal to your program. Bark and other natural materials are easy to work with, and provide instant gratification through a creative project. Collecting bark can lead to a learning experience, since clients have the opportunity to learn to identify different trees by their bark and cones.

## Materials

Natural materials, such as small blocks of birch bark wood, approximately 4 x 12 inches (10 x 30.25 cm); 2 x 3 inch (7.55 x 5 cm) pieces of birch bark; approximately 4 x 12 inches (10 x 30.5 cm) bark pieces from dead trees or wood piles; drieds such as strawflowers, grasses, small hydrangea heads, statice, lavender, larkspur and yarrow.

**Other**

Florist picks, ribbon, florist's tape and wire, ribbon for bows, 12-inch (30.5 cm) tapered candles, artificial bird, small silk flowers for accent, lacquer, sahara oasis, glue gun, wire cutters, scissors, a knife and a drill.

**Procedure for Table Design**

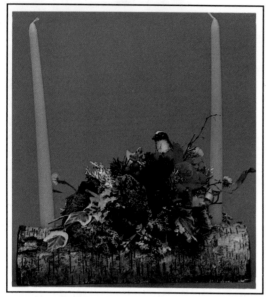

Step 1: This project uses a birch bark log cut in half. Choose a block of wood 4 x 12 inches (10 x 30.5 cm) long, approximately 2 inches (5 cm) thick. Make sure the wood is clean and that the white of the bark is visible. Brush off any dirt and sand rough edges.

Step 2: If you wish to place candles into this design, drill holes into the wood and position them either in the middle or to the sides.

Step 3: After the candle has been secured, glue on a 2-inch (5 cm) square piece of sahara.

Step 4: Cover the oasis with Spanish moss, and firm with greening pins or cut-up florist's wire into small sections and fashion into small "hair" pins. Push these pins into the sahara, to secure the moss.

Step 5: Where you have placed the sahara oasis will determine the shape of the composition. Generally, the finished design should radiate evenly across the surface of the wood. Begin by placing a bow into the middle of the oasis. If you have a florist pick with a variety of small flower heads and berries, cut each stem and wire and tape them in and around the bow area. Remember to cut all the ends of dried material at a 45 degree angle to prevent stems from breaking when they are pierced into the floral foam. Fill in the design with small hydrangea heads, using them as leaves to give the design a good base. After you have used enough drieds and accents, feather the design with *Gypsophila* (Baby's Breath) to give it an airy look and complement the wood.

Step 6: Add a small bird or ornament to complement the design and season.

Step 7: Spray the finished piece with a thin coating of clear lacquer.

**Procedure for Small Candle Designs**

These designs will complement the above arrangements or provide a small candle design. Begin by using a small 3 x 2 inch (7.5 x 5 cm) round piece of birch bark wood. Either drill a hole for a candle, or hot-glue on a small candle holder. The method of the design can be a smaller version of the above project or design a small corsage made from the same materials as above. Glue moss around the candle area and fasten the corsage to complete the candle design.

**Procedure for Wall Design Using Bark**

Step 1: Choose a rugged piece of maple or birch bark approximately 3 x 12 inches (7.5 x 30.5 cm) in size. Brush off any dirt and remove any broken or crumbling parts.

Step 2: Drill a small hole in the top of the plaque to hang the finished design.

Step 3: Glue on a small piece of sahara oasis approximately 2 inches square (5 cm) and 2 inches (5 cm) from the bottom, leaving equal space on either side.

Step 4: Cover the oasis with Spanish moss and secure. For a balanced look, the design should radiate up to the top of the bark leaving at least 2 inches (5 cm) of space from the edge.

Step 5: Begin by using tall drieds, approximately 6-8 inches (15-20 cm) long. Cut the stems at a 45 degree angle and push them in to give your design height and a backdrop. Choose colours to complement the design or use a monochromatic colour scheme. Place or stage your flower heads into threes, and have them at different heights. Fill in with drieds and other material in different heights to give balance and depth. Reindeer moss adds a natural look to this arrangement, and you can hot-glue or pin the moss into the oasis.

Step 6: Add a small bow and a bird to round out the design.

Step 7: Spray the design with a clear lacquer to preserve all materials and to prevent flower heads and grasses from falling apart.

## Therapeutic Application

These wood or bark designs provide your program with an inexpensive activity. The style of the design determines the time of season or special event. Natural products are easy to work with and the results provide instant gratification. Be creative and use what ever material you find: dried grasses, twigs and weeds add a rustic look and provide texture to complement the bark.

Twig Bundle

## Grapevine Designs

(A) Grapevine Wreaths  (B) Swag or Garland Designs (C) Twig Bundles.

Purpose:  To teach clients how to collect, dry and design on grapevines.

Population:  Ideal for clients who can safely do a nature walk, or for clients who can handle a graded or two-step procedure, i.e. sorting and tying bundles.

Background: Collecting grapevines provides an excellent opportunity to get outside and enjoy nature. Grapevines can be found in thickets, along the borders of woods, or trailing over bushes or climbing trees.  Collecting can be done from early May to late November.  The time period offers you a range of seasons to explore and experience the changes in nature: spring flowers, summer fragrances, and the colourful leaves and bounty of the fall.  Many clients enjoy working with grapevines, as it is a natural medium that provides a great base for a variety of projects.  These designs are ideal for developing good use of leisure time and the results are appreciated as gifts or decorations to beautify a home or living quarters.

## Materials

Grapevines:  *Vitis labrusca* (Northern Fox Grape or Plum Grape).  Collect from early May to late November.

Sahara Oasis:  Size is determined by the shape of the grapevine design.

Ribbon:  The ribbon sets the stage for the colour and number of materials to be used.  I suggest using a "French country" or "Victorian style", as it provides you with lots of colour and eliminates the use of a number of flowers.  For Christmas, use a variety of coloured, velvet ribbon to provide a rich-looking, design.  Select ribbon that has a good coating of sizing to help keep loops full-looking.  For a large bow consisting of approximately 10 loops, choose a ribbon width of 2 1/2 inches (6.5 cm).  For smaller shapes, cut the ribbon in half lengthwise, and make the bow size complement the dimensions of the grapevine design.  Always purchase bolts of ribbon wholesale.

Flowers:  Use wild flowers or flowers and herbs that you have grown and dried in your program.  This will cut costs and provide good quality and quantity of material.

Perennials:  *Physalis alkekengi franchetti* (Chinese Lantern) (seed head), *Delphinium, Achillea mille-folium* (Yarrow), *Artemisia, Echinops bannaticus* (Globe Thistle) (seed head), *Hydrangea, Echinacea* (Purple Coneflower) (seed head), *Gypsophila elegans* (Baby's Breath), *Limonium tatarica atifolium* (Sea Lavender), *Rosa sp.* (Rose), *Gomphrena globosa* (Globe Amaranth), *Paeonia lactiflora* (Peony) and *Dianthus* (Carnation).

Herbs: *Lavandula spica* (Lavender), *Salvia labiatae sp* (Sage), *Linum sp* (Flax), *Labiatae* (Mint), *Salvia labiatae sp* (Salvia), *Galium odoratum* (Sweet Woodruff), *Thymus vulgaris* (Thyme).

Annuals: *Salvia farinacea "Victoria"* (Blue Salvia), *Delphinium consolida* (Larkspur), *Helichrysum bracteatum* (Strawflower), *Limonium sinuaton* (Statice), *Gomphrena globosa* (Globe Amaranth) (seed head).

Biennials: *Lunaria* (Honesty), *Molucella laevis* (Bells of Ireland).

Wild flowers: Blackeyed Susan, Dock, Cattails, Milkweed pods, Pampas grass, Queen Anne's Lace, Goldenrod, Teasel, Thistle, Joe-Pye Weed, Loosestrife, Pearly Everlasting.

Other: There are a number of silk or parchment flowers and leaves available through wholesale florist supply companies.

Cones and Nuts: Small spruce cones, acorns or chestnuts.

Other: Florist tape, wire, Spanish moss.

Glue Gun: Use small, low-temperature glue gun.

Secateurs: You will need a good pair of pruning shears.

Miscellanous: Thick garden gloves will protect hands, and a large sturdy laundry bag for carrying vines (plastic rips too easily) and ceramic tile adhesive.

## Procedure for Making and Drying the Grapevine Forms

Step 1: ·Once you have located the grapevines, pull or cut long pieces of the vine from the trees or bushes. Removing the grapevines from other plant material usually saves the life of the plant, as the grapevine tends to choke out everything on which it grows. Grapevines should be stripped of leaves; grapes and tendrils can be left on for character.

Step 2:

" Making a Wreath Form: Begin by making a 12-15 inch (30.5-38 cm) circle with the vines. Wind vines in and out and around in a circular motion to give a woven look. Continue this procedure until you have the desired thickness and shape. Stretch the wreath at different points to keep it round.

" Garland or Arch Form: Strip the leaves from the vines. Choose six branches about 3-4 feet (91-122 cm) long, and determine the size of the design by the length of the vines. Divide branches into three sets of two and braid the pieces together to get a woven effect. Cut off end pieces to give a finished edge. To make a small arch, simply cut the circular wreath form in half, to create two semi-circles. To secure, wrap wire around each swag in three places.

" Twig Bundles: This is the easiest method. Once you have removed the leaves, cut the grapevines into pieces of approximately 6 inches (15.5 cm) in length. Cut the branches the desired length. The thickness is determined by the number of sticks you put together. Wire the bundle together by wrapping florist wire within one inch (2.5 cm) of each end.

Step 3: Hang grapevine forms in a warm, dry area for approximately two weeks. Tighten wires to allow for shrinkage.

## Procedure for Designing Gravevine Forms

Designing these three projects is done in the same manner. The only difference is the size and amount of material used. To encourage a theme, completed designs can be displayed on a table, wall or over a picture.

Step 1: For clients who cannot work with a glue gun, prepare a form by hot-gluing a piece of sahara oasis onto the grapevine frame. This provides a base for the design material. The size of sahara used is determined by the style and the amount of material you wish to use. For those who can safely work with a glue gun, it is not necessary to use oasis. Instead, glue all pieces onto the grapevine form. Another method is to make a large corsage-like design and wire this piece onto the wreath frame.

Step 2: When designing, keep all material within the balance of the frame or base. The design technique used for all projects is similar. If you are using dry floral foam, cover this with Spanish moss, then cut small pieces of wire into 2-inch (5 cm) lengths, bend in half (like a hairpin) and push into the oasis securing moss in place. Begin all designs by attaching the bow; determine the style of the bow by the shape of the design. Teaching the art of bow-making is a very difficult task, requiring a great deal of patience and skill. To make this situation easier, either use a paper ribbon that is simple to fabricate into a bow, or buy a ready-made one. I make all the bows ahead of time, to save money and prevent frustration. If you wish to teach bow-making, make sure clients are high functioning so they will be able to perform the skills needed without experiencing a great degree of frustration. After the bow is either glued onto the frame, pushed into the sahara, work all pieces from this area.

Step 3: Use green silk leaves or dried herbs, such as sage, or treated cedar pieces. Affix these pieces under the bow and radiate them out from either side of the bow. This gives you a green base from which to work.

Step 4: Select your colour scheme. This is determined by the colour of the bow. For wreaths and arches, glue in at least three larger flowers in and around the bow area. If your bow is as small as the twig bundle, then choose at least six small flower heads (small ribbon roses are ideal for this design).

Step 5: This is the stage where you will accent your design with all the small drieds. Use small pieces of larkspur, statice, hydrangea, baby's breath, lavender, or whatever you feel will blend in and around the bow. Extend these drieds to either side of the bow to give length and depth to the design. Glue these pieces over the green base so colours blend homogeneously, filling in any spaces to achieve a full look.

Step 6: For the finishing touches use miniature cones or small pieces of herbs for fragrance and colour in the grapevines.

Step 7: When the design is completed, add a bird and small nest, shaped from moss. Miniature mushroom birds will complement the twig bundles beautifully.

Step 8: To hang the wreath or arch, attach a small florist wire to the back of the design.

### Therapeutic Application

These designs can be made for all seasonal events and can also be used as bazaar items. Grapevines are an inexpensive material that provide a base for many horticulturally-related crafts. Take your time in making these forms and designing them. These projects should be broken down into a number of classes. Small stones or wooden clothes pins can be substituted for the twig bundle base.

These classes should be taught using a guided approach demonstrating and working on each step with the client. For clients who may need support, staff and volunteers should be assisting them in reaching each stage through verbal encouragement and positive feedback. It is important to teach fundamental design techniques, but if clients wish to vary from this and do their own style, this shows creativity and initiative. Working with these kinds of projects requires good resource strategies in that all material must be organized ahead of time. Your methodology and approach in teaching these skills will ensure success.

## Alternative Methods

When designing the grapevine wreaths, an alternative style is to use herbs or natural weeds, such as Goldenrod, Queen Anne's Lace and Tansy. For herbal wreaths, cut a variety of strong-smelling herbs approximately 4-5 inches (10-12.5 cm) long. Begin by making a small bundle of herbs. Place them on the front of the wreath; wrap with wire, and then overlap the stems with the next herb. Continue this pattern until the entire wreath is filled. Tuck in any loose ends and add a bow with tails. Hang to dry in a kitchen or other area that will allow the fragrance to permeate the air. To make a natural looking wreath, simply insert the yellow tansy or goldenrod flower heads between the woven grapevines, start at one end and overlap each piece, so that the whole wreath forms a yellow base. When finished, insert the Queen Anne's Lace and Tansy at intervals to give an even pattern. Let dry and decorate with a bow.

## *Combination Plantings*

(A) Tropical Gardens  (B) Cacti Gardens

Purpose:  To design and grow a variety of plants in containers.

Population: (AL), (D), (Scz), (AD), (AN), (CI).

Background:  Growing a variety of plants in special containers provides clients with an interesting collection of plants, while at the same time eliminating the need for many small pots. The finished product provides interest by its multidimensional shape, size and variety. The containers are ideal as gifts, because of the diversity of plant materials and creative styles.

### Materials

Containers:  Plastic or clay pots, baskets, ceramic dishes, glass containers (coffee jars or designer glass bowls).

Growing Medium:  Equal parts soil, peatmoss, perlite or a soilless mix.

Plants:  Determine the varieties of plants you wish to grow by the light source available and the style of garden you wish to plant, i.e. tropical or cactus).  Choose plants that are compatible and provide a variety of colour, texture, shapes and sizes.

1. Tropical plants for a low light area (no direct sunlight):
   *Aglaonema* (Chinese Evergreen), *Dracaena* (Corn Plant), *Fittonia* (Nerve Plant), *Ferns*, *Helixine* (Baby Tears), *Maranta* (Prayer Plant), *Philodendron, Sansevieria* (Snake Plant), *Spathiphyllum* (White Flag), *Scindapsus* (Heart Leaf Climbers).

2. Tropical plants for a medium light (east window):
   *Chlorophytum* (Spider Plant), *Cordyline* (Ti Plant), *Euonymus, Ficus* (Weeping Fig), *Gynura* (Velvet Plant), *Impatiens, Kalanchoe, Peperomia, Saintpaulia* (African Violet), *Tradescantia* (Wandering Jew), *Begonia* and *Coleus*.

3. High light area (southern exposure; during the summer periods, protect plants from the hot sun):
   *Acacia* (Mimosa), *Aphelandra* (Zebra Plant), *Bougainvillea* (Paper Flower), *Citrus* (Orange, Lemon), *Codiaeum* (Croton), *Hibiscus, Hoya* (Wax Plant) and *Iresine* (Blood Leaf).

4. Cacti and succulents; these plants require high light and can be planted together as they are compatible: *Aporocatuac flagelliformis* (Rat's Tail Cactus), *Chamascereus silvestrii* (Peanut Cactus), *Cereus peruvianus monstrosus* (Rock Cactus), *Echinofossulocactus zacatecasensis* (Brain Cactus), *Echinocactus grusonii* (Barrel Cactus), *Gymnocalycium mihanovichii var. friedrichii* (Red Capped Cactus), Golden Lily Cactus, *Lovivia aurea*.

5. Succulents: *Aeonium tabulaeforme* (Saucer Plant), Agave *filifera* (Thread Agave), *Aloe aristata* (Lace Aloe), *Crassula argentea* (Jade Plant)*, Crassula lycopodiodes* (Rat Tail Plant, *Crassula perforata* (String of Buttons), *Crassula rochea var. falcata* (Propeller Plant), *Echeveria derenbergi* (Painted Lady)*, Echeveria setosa* (Firecracker Plant), *Haworthia margaritifera* (Pearl Plant), *Kalanchoe tomentosa,* (Panda Plant), *Sedum pachyphyllum* (Jelly Beans).

**Optional Material**
Coloured gravel, tongue depressors, small branch, artificial birds, Spanish moss, reindeer moss, ribbon to complement container, small rocks, driftwood in a variety of sizes, florist picks for season accent, i.e. Happy Easter, Merry Christmas). Be creative and come up with your own accents.

**Procedure**
Step 1: Decide what kind of container garden you wish to create and grow. Tropical plants are ideal for plastic pots, baskets and glass containers; shallow ceramic dishes complement the texture and characteristics of cacti and succulents.

Step 2: The size of the container will be determined by the number and size of plants you use. A 6-inch (15.2 cm) container will hold approximately 4-5 inch (10-12.5 cm) pots. Be careful not to over-plant, and allow the plants to fill in where possible.

Step 3: Determine how you would like the finished design to look by arranging the plants beside the container. Tall plants can be located in the middle, while bushy plants and trailing varieties can be planted around the sides of the container.

Step 4: Fill the bottom of the container with approximately 1 inch (2.5 cm) of drainage material. If the container has holes, cover the perforations with small pebbles or clay chips to allow moisture to drain away from the pot. For special containers (ceramic bowls, glass containers and baskets) that do not have drainage holes, it is essential to fill the bottom with drainage material to prevent plants from rotting. When planting a coffee jar, you can fill it half-full with sections of perlite and coloured gravel to create a "sundae" effect.

Step 5: Begin by filling the container with the growing medium to within 1 inch (2.5 cm) of the rim. Dig the holes, and then remove the plant you are going to use from its pot by turning it upside down and gently tapping it out of the container. For large tropical plants, remove some of the soil mass, so the plant fits into the container. When working with plants that have spines or sharp edges, such as cacti and succulents, wear gloves and wrap the plants with heavy newspaper to prevent injury.

Step 6: Firm down the soil around each plant to secure it into place.

Step 7: To accent the design of the container garden, push in a branch or piece of driftwood. You can also add a bow, artificial bird or pick to give it a festive look. Complete the design by filling in the soil area with coloured gravel or Spanish moss.

Step 8: Desert gardens should only contain cactus and succulent varieties. To accent the desert garden, use a spoon to firm the soil around each plant, so that the surface area is flat. After planting, separate plant areas into sections by pressing tongue depressors, with the narrow edge up, into the soil. Make sure the tongue depressors cross the container to form sections in or around each plant. Fill each section with coloured gravel, and then gently remove the sticks. Add a small piece of driftwood, reindeer moss and rocks to give the design an arid appearance.

## Care of the Container Garden

Watering: Use room temperature water to promote even growth and prevent plants from being shocked by cold water. Moisten each plant individually, so that the moisture reaches the roots. Be careful not to over-water, as most of these containers do not have drainage holes. Repeat this procedure when the soil appears dry. Water well once a month, allowing the soil area to dry out completely between waterings.

Light and Temperature: Container gardens can be placed in appropriate light according to the variety of plants used. Low-light tropical dish gardens prefer a north and east exposure; medium-light tropical plants prefer a southern exposure. For cacti gardens, place plants in a southern or western direction. During the summer periods, provide some shade to guard plants against the hot sun. During the winter months, do not let plants sit in a cold window during the night.

Fertilizer: Plants can have a little fertilizer to keep them healthy, but not too much because that causes them to grow out of their containers. Use an all-purpose, water soluble fertilizer such as 20-20-20. Fertilize once every two months. Fertilize cacti and succulents in the spring and summer only.

Pruning: Some plants will grow taller than others, and appear leggy. Cut off these branches or growing tips with a pair of scissors. This procedure will keep plants bushy and within balance. Remove any dead leaves.

Insects and Diseases: Choose only healthy plants to prevent any problems. Spray plants once a month with Safer's soap or use a swab dipped in alcohol to kill insects. To grow plants successfully, always provide proper growing conditions, such as temperature and ventilation. Close observation will keep you alert to any problem that may arise. If the plant appears not to be growing properly, immediately cut off the affected area; use a chemical or fungicide if needed and follow proper growing conditions.

Repotting: When plants start to grow out of the container and lose their effectiveness, remove them from the dish and plant them into an appropriate pot size. Remember that all container gardens will eventually need repotting.

## Therapeutic Application

Combination plantings are great projects for teaching clients how to grow a variety of compatible plants in one container. This activity provides an exercise in creative design and also the care and culture of plants. The finished product makes an ideal gift suitable for all occasions.

## Herb Vinegars

Purpose: To make herb vinegars for culinary use.

Population: This project can be broken down to meet the needs of all populations.

Background: Working with fresh herbs and vinegars is a great way to stimulate the senses providing a two-fold purpose: collecting the material and making the vinegars. Herbal vinegars were used in the nineteenth century for medicinal purposes, such as tonics and digestive aids, and to complement special food dishes. The aroma of fresh herbs can stimulate the memory and provide clients with a wonderful taste and smell sensation. This project can be done as soon as the herbs emerge from the ground.

### Materials

Herbs: Sage, mint, basil, chives, marjoram, thyme, tarragon, garlic, oregano, parsley, lavender, lemon balm, dill.

Vinegars: Red wine, cider, white wine.

Spices: Caraway seed, cloves.

Fruit: Lemons or limes.

Containers: Clear glass fruit juice or soft drink bottles.

Equipment: Small funnels, corks to fit the bottles (available at most wine making stores), a knife or pair of scissors, rubber or surgical gloves.

### Herb Vinegars Recipes

Because of our populations and for safety reasons, we do not boil the vinegar as is usually done in conventional recipes. We treat these the same way as making sun tea, allowing the sun to provide the heat and give flavour to the vinegar.

Mint (Spearmint, Peppermint, Citrus) and white vinegar: This combination is used for a fresh fruit salad and as a sauce for roast lamb.

Sage and red wine vinegar: This combination is used as a marinade for pork chops, roast pork and as a spicy dressing for rice salad.

Lavender and white wine vinegar: This combination is used to flavour stewed fruit and can replace liqueur in some desserts.

Chive and caraway in white wine vinegar: This blend is great for a tangy coleslaw.

Basil, marjoram, thyme, tarragon in red wine vinegar: This four-herb vinegar is an excellent dressing for fresh green salads.

Dill, lemon, garlic, parsley and white wine vinegar: You can use this mixture for any fish dish.

Mint and white vinegar: Use as a dressing for new potatoes.

Basil, garlic, oregano and cider vinegar: Can be used as a vinaigrette for freshly sliced garden tomatoes.

Tarragon, cloves, garlic, cider vinegar: An excellent combination for a spinach salad.

Garlic and white wine vinegar: This is an excellent combination to keep on hand as the base for dressings.

## Procedure

Step 1: Always collect the herbs in the morning. Make sure they are free of insects and any discolouration in the leaves. Cut stems approximately 3-4 inches (7.5 cm-10 cm) long.

Rinse herbs in cold water and dry in a clean towel, or spin dry in a salad spinner.

Step 2: Bottles should be washed and all labels removed. To sterilize containers, either put through a dishwasher or pour boiling water into the glass and rinse. This activity should be done by staff or those individuals who can safely handle working with boiling water.

Step 3: Corks should be soaked in warm water for 1 hour to absorb moisture.

Step 4: Begin class preparation by asking the clients which recipe they would like to use. (See recipes.)

Step 5: Clients should wear rubber or surgical gloves when working with fresh herbs.

Step 6: After herbs have been inserted into the bottles, use a funnel to fill the bottle with vinegar. This task can be done in pairs, with one person holding the bottle and funnel, while the other pours vinegar into the bottle. Fill the container to within 1 inch (2.5 cm) of the top and push cork into the bottle so the liquid touches the bottom of the cork.

Step 7: The finished product can be placed in a sunny window for one month, to help the herbs blend into the vinegar. However, vinegars with chive heads or basil should not be put into the sun, or the rich colours of the herbs will not stay in the vinegar.

Step 8: Tie a small card listing the ingredients around the neck of the bottle. Making the cards is an activity that can be done ahead.

Step 9: The final stage also should be done by responsible staff and clients. After one month, seal the vinegar by dipping the cork into melted wax. For colour, add a non-toxic wax crayon to the wax.

Finished products are great bazaar items that can be decorated with a piece of fabric and tied with a ribbon. All bottles should have a recipe card attached. The beautiful colour of the herbal vinegars makes a great window display and they are ideal for gift baskets. There are no additives or preservatives in these recipes and they will last up to one year. For use in salads, mix equal parts of herbal vinegar with oil, and add sugar to taste.

## *Miniature Glass Ball Terrarium*

Purpose: To create a living Christmas tree ornament.
Population: Those clients who have good eyesight and can handle fine motor skill tasks.
Background: This project helps clients learn about growing plants, and provides a unique Christmas tree ornament.

### Materials
Clear glass Christmas tree balls (ornaments usually purchased in different colours); small paper funnel; plastic coffee stir stick; small 2 1/2 inch (6 cm) clay pot to rest ornament on when it is being planted; red and green aquarium gravel; misting bottle; cuttings from small plants suitable for growing in a terrarium, e.g., *Fittonia* (Nerve Plant), *Pilea, Euonymus, Pilea nummularifolia* (Creeping Charlie), *Pilea depressa* (miniature leaf *Peperomia*).

### Procedure
Step 1: If you have purchased coloured glass ornaments, use great care in cleaning them. Wear rubber gloves and prepare ornaments by removing metal caps and soaking them in bleach for three hours. Carefully remove ornaments from the bleach and rinse with clear water. If a haze exists on the glass, use a Q-Tip and gently remove paint or haze. Rinse in warm water and dry.
Step 2: Begin by resting the glass bubble onto the clay pot while you spoon a little perlite down a small paper funnel into the container. Fill the glass with approximately one half inch (.7 cm) of this material and then top with 1/4 inch (.5 cm) of coloured gravel, red or green, or both.
Step 3: Top with 1 inch (2.5 cm) soilless mix.
Step 4: Decide where you would like the cuttings to be planted and dig a small hole with the stir stick.
Step 5: Drop the small cutting down the opening by gently angling and sliding it into the hole prepared for it. Press the cutting firmly into place and tamp to hold into place. Repeat this procedure with each cutting. Do not use more than four cuttings.
Step 6: Water the plants with a jet of water. Do not fill the bottom of the ornament with water; instead use just enough water to keep the growing medium moist.

Step 7: Glue the lid back onto the container to prevent the weight of the terrarium from pulling the cap off.

Step 8: Hang completed ornament onto a tree branch by using a small piece of florist's wire.

## Application

This project is limited to a population who can handle the number of fine skills involved. The ornament makes an excellent item for bazaars and lasts long into the winter months.

## Potpourri

Purpose:  Making a fragrant potpourri for use in many projects.

Population:  All populations.  This can provide a variety of step procedures.

Background:  What is potpourri?  It is a mixture of decorative ingredients, such as dried flower heads, petals, herbs, and wood curls, with materials, such as spices, fixatives and oils added. Colour, shape and fragrance are provided by the flowers, petals herbs and wood chips.  Adding spices complements and enhances the fragrance.  The fixative will absorb and hold the scent of the plants. Essential oils help season the mixture and encourage a long-lived scent.

In the past, potpourri was traditionally used for masking unpleasant odours.  The perfume of these mixtures, carried in elaborately jewelled pomander balls by the nobility, or scattered onto the floor so that the aromatic scent of rosemary and sweet woodruff was released when trodden upon, captured the redolence of the garden. Nowadays potpourri is used to sweeten areas in homes and facilities.

Making potpourri through a natural art form exposes clients to many types of plant material and gives them a variety of step procedures, from simple to more complex. Potpourri-making is also an enjoyable activity, which can stimulate the senses and lead to many other projects.

### Materials

Dried Plant Material:  Flower heads or petals such as rose, pansy, delphinium, tulip, lavender, forsythia, marigold, chrysanthemum, statice.  The possibilities are endless!

Herbs:  Lavender, mint, sweet woodruff, scented geranium, lemon balm, basil, rosemary, sage, etc.

Powdered Spices:  Cinnamon, ginger, allspice, cloves, cardamon.

Fixatives:  Powdered orris root, gum benzoin or cornstarch (non-poisonous).

Essential Oils:  Rose, lemon grass, pine, tangerine, lavender, vanilla.

Other:  Other materials I have found useful are dried orange and lemon peel for a citron potpourri; cedar; small cones and dried berries for seasonal expression and fragrance; small wood curls from the planings of pine and cedar to add depth, bulk and colour.  These shavings or curls are easy to dye, by mixing them into a pan of water with one ounce of food colouring.  For a rich or dark colour, add more food colouring.  Dry in open boxes lined with paper towels.

Containers and Tools:  Large metal mixing bowls, long-handled spoons, rubber gloves, and large pickle jars with lids (for storing ingredients until ready to use).

## Procedure

All plant material to be used must be dried thoroughly to prevent moulding and spoilage. (See ***Drying Herbs and Flowers***). Pressed flower heads can be used as well as those dried by the usual methods. Begin by deciding what kind of potpourri to make. There are many kinds and mixtures, and you will soon discover how to produce your own blend. Start with a basic recipe, such as the one for rose or lavender potpourri.

## Rose or Lavender Potpourri

Step 1:  For a rose potpourri, use one quart of dried rose petals and leaves; substitute lavender flowers and petals for lavender.

Step 2:  For rose potpourri use one cup dried small rose heads; for lavender use lavender flowers or dried purple statice heads.

Step 3:  Add three cups of dried herbs such as mint, sweet marjoram or lemon balm.

Step 4:  Three cups of dyed wood curls (red, green or mauve).

Step 5:  Three tablespoons of cinnamon and ground nutmeg.

Step 6:  Three quarters of a cup of orris root.

Step 7:  Four ounces of rose oil, or four ounces of lavender oil.

Mix together all ingredients except the rose or lavender oil. After the mixture is blended, add the oil and mix thoroughly. Store in a large pickle jar, marked with the date and variety of mix; keep in a warm dry place for six weeks. Shake the jar frequently to help blend and strengthen the mixture.

## Application

The above mixture can be used in a variety of projects. To stimulate interest and provide fragrance, place potpourri in large, attractive, shallow bowls, baskets or display saucers and locate them near entrances and areas of traffic.

## Potpourri Projects

Sachets:  These bags are ideal for special events such as bazaars and weddings. To make them, simply cut out a 10-inch (25.5 cm) piece of fabric and empty a 2-inch (5 cm) pot of potpourri into the middle. Draw up the four corners of fabric and tie with coordinating ribbon. To add a name tag, simply punch a hole into the tag, slip onto the ribbon, and tie with a bow to secure it in place. To add colour and dimension, insert a small, taped flower (with stem and leaves) through the ribbon; curl the stem by wrapping the wire around a pencil.

Try this unique potpourri for cat enthusiasts, using a combination of catnip and mint. Place mixture into a sturdy fabric with a cat picture or design, fold up corners and tie tightly with a strong piece of co-ordinating yarn.

Wicker containers make ideal potpourri holders. Put potpourri into small wicker containers, close the lid and attach a corsage to the lid for a festive look.

For a Christmas tree ornament, fill a clear plastic or glass ornament with potpourri, tie with coordinating bow and hang onto a tree branch.

To make a potpourri wreath, either tie small bags of potpourri onto the wreath, or simply paint the wreath with white glue and dip it into potpourri so that it is completely covered. Add a bow for the final touch.

Cover an embroidery hoop with a piece of netting or lace; fill the netting or lace with potpourri and cover with another piece of material. Clamp together the second ring (or hoop) onto the first hoop and secure it tightly. Cut off excess material and add a small bow or edge it with lace. ❧

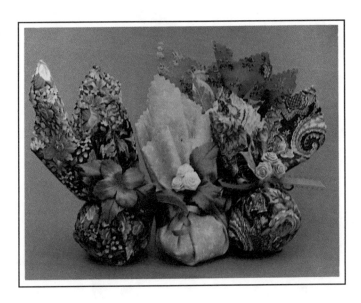

**Calligraphy Messages**
Shown below are several calligraphy messages that may be used in your stationery and greeting card program.

Friend

Good Luck

God bless

Good Bye

Best Wishes

Happy Valentine's Day

# *Horticultural Therapy Training*

Unfortunately, there are no degree programs in Canada in horticultural therapy. The Canadian Horticultural Therapy Association (CHTA) does, however, offer many workshops and training sessions for persons interested in learning about this discipline.

The American Horticultural Therapy Association (AHTA) provides support education and professional registration for its members. This association is affiliated with institutions offering degree programs in horticultural therapy. This governing body also provides two professional classifications for horticultural therapists: The Horticultural Therapist Registered (HTR), is for those who have completed a degree in Horticultural Therapy plus a one-year internship. The Horticultural Therapist Masters (HTM), is for horticultural therapists who have finished graduate work in this field, have worked extensively in horticultural therapy and have acquired additional training or professional achievements. Registration is voluntary and there are no licensing laws.

For information contact:
American Horticultural Therapy Association (AHTA),
909 York Street,
Denver, Colorado, USA 80206
(303) 331-3862

Universities and Colleges currently offering horticultural therapy programs or courses:
Kansas State University, Kansas
Herbert H. Lehman College, New York
Texas A & M University, Texas
University of Rhode Island, Rhode Island

**CHAPTER**

# 20

# *Resources*

T he following resources will assist you in finding a variety of sources for material to use in your horticultural therapy program. They include Professional Organizations, Allied Health Care Associations, Voluntary Associations, Reference Materials and Suppliers.

## *Professional Organizations*

**CANADIAN HORTICULTURAL THERAPY ASSOCIATION (CHTA)**
c/o Mitchell Hewson HTM
70 Westmount Road
Guelph, Ontario
Canada N1H 5H8

The largest professional organization in Canada is the Canadian Horticultural Therapy Association (CHTA). This organization networks throughout Canada, providing workshops, newsletters and resources for learning about the use of horticulture as a therapeutic medium. To assist members there is a resource binder of material on projects, plant care and related information. Members consist of registered horticultural therapists, recreation and occupational therapists, horticulturists, nurses, educators and other personnel who work in a variety of institutions and health care facilities. Workshops are given on a variety of topics for interested staff who work with special populations. Content may include hands-on practical information for growing plants, related horticultural projects, and therapeutic application of horticulture when working with clients with special needs. These day-long workshops and seminars are held once per year. The CHTA executive networks with all of its members to keep up-to-date with their needs, and provides ongoing support in their pursuit of horticulture as a therapy. Annual membership fee is $25.00.

## DIGA—DISABLED INDEPENDENT GARDENERS ASSOCIATION

1632 Sutherland Avenue
North Vancouver, BC V7L 4B7
Canada

This organization assists people who are disabled and older adults to pursue gardening despite the barriers of age, physical limitations and environment. It connects people who need help with resources, products, facilities and other related information needed to foster an interest in gardening. A newsletter is published and workshops provided on a variety of topics relating to gardening and special needs. Members are professionals, similar to that of the CHTA, who contribute valuable resources to beginning or continuing gardeners regardless of limitations or special needs. Annual membership fee is $15.00.

## AMERICAN HORTICULTURAL THERAPY ASSOCIATION (AHTA)

362A Christopher Avenue,
Gaithersburg, Maryland 20879
USA

The AHTA has the largest body of practising registered Horticultural Therapists. This organization has over 750 members, who work in a variety of facilities. The AHTA holds a major conference once a year, providing colleagues and interested persons with an excellent agenda on the field and scope of horticultural therapy.

The conference permits therapists and persons working in the field of horticultural therapy to network and share the latest findings and assessments available in the field. This conference also provides an excellent vehicle for promoting the excellent work done by individuals working in this discipline, through the recognition of their talents and services. Annual awards and scholarships are given to deserving people for their humanitarian and professional services. The Douglas J. Schwartz Greenhouse grants programs, administered by the AHTA, awards numerous greenhouses to outstanding institutions and agencies for their need and desire to further horticulture as a therapy.

The AHTA facilitates a national employment project for persons with disabilities. Guidance is given to educational facilities in setting-up programs and practicums for students in horticultural therapy. They provide a wealth of resources, i.e., published material such as journals, books, papers and newsletters. Annual membership directories help members network with others who work with similar populations and agencies. There are also audio visual materials available to help further the scope and practice of this profession. Annual membership fee is $35.00 US

**HORTICULTURAL THERAPY SOCIETY (England)**
Goulds Ground
Vallis Way, Frome
Somerset, BAll3DW
United Kingdom

This association prints a quarterly newsletter called "Growth Point" for gardeners with special needs. It offers a great deal of information about horticultural therapy in Britain. They may list a number of resources, training available, projects and editorials on individuals who have benefited from gardening. Some sections include "Bookshelf", reviews of books available on a variety of horticultural subjects; "Toolbox", information on tools and equipment, products, etc. A well-written and illustrated magazine. Annual membership fee is 12 pounds sterling.

## *Allied Health Care Associations*

**National Office Canada**—Alzheimer Society of Canada
1320 Yonge Street, Suite 302
Toronto, Ontario M4T 1X2
Canada

**National Eating Disorder**
Information Centre
200 Elizabeth Street
Toronto, Ontario M5G 2C4
Canada

**Schizophrenic Society of Canada**
814-75 The Donway West
Don Mills, Ontario M3C 2E9
Canada

**Addiction Research Foundation**
33 Russell Street
Toronto, Ontario M5S 2S1
Canada

**Affective Disorders Unit**
Clarke Institute of Psychiatry
250 College Street,
Toronto, Ontario M5T 1R8
Canada

**National Depressive & Manic Depressive Association**
53W Jackson Boulevard
Room 618,
Chicago, Illinois 60604
USA

**Alzheimer Diseases International**
70 East Lake Street, Suite 600
Chicago Illinois, 60601
USA

**National Association of Anorexia with Associated Disorders**
P.O. Box 7
Highland Park, Ilinois 60035
USA

**National Alliance for the Mentally Ill**
1901 North Fort Myer Drive
Suite 500
Arlington, Virginia 22209
USA

**National Association of State, Alcohol with Drug Abuse, Directors**
Suite 530
444 North Capitol Street N.W.
Washington, D.C. 20001
USA

## *Voluntary Associations*

The following associations can help you organize and set up a volunteer program:

**Canada-Wide Volunteer Ontario**
2 Dunbloor Road
Suite 203
Etobicoke, Ontario M9A 2E4
Canada
(416) 236-0588

This number will also give you information on the Canadian Association of Volunteer Bureaus and Centres for volunteer bureaus in your area.

**American Volunteer Association (AVA)**
Boulder, Colorado 80306
USA

## *Reference Materials*

I have found the following books most helpful when researching information for programs and program content:

GARDENING AS THERAPY: A RESOURCE MANUAL FOR DEVELOPMENT OF HORTICUL-TURAL THERAPY PROGRAMS. Four volumes: "For the Spring Season"; "For the Summer Season"; "For the Fall Season" and "For the Winter Season".
The Botanical Garden
The University of British Columbia
6501 N.W. Marine Drive
Vancouver, B.C. V6T 1W5
Canada

The first two volumes are out of print, but all these books may be republished in one volume in the near future. Content includes: outdoor and indoor gardening, plants, projects, garden plans, flower arranging, etc. These are practical manuals that will help you get started, with easy illustrations and step procedures. Cost $4.95 each.

Rothert, Eugene A. Jr. and Daubert, James R. HORTICULTURAL THERAPY FOR SENIOR CENTERS NURSING HOMES RETIREMENT LIVING and HORTICULTURAL THERAPY AT A PSYCHIATRIC HOSPITAL. Cost $10.00.
Chicago Horticultural Society,
PO Box 400
Glencoe, Illinois 60022
USA

These two books provide a general overview of working with older adults and psychiatric patients in their own environment. Emphasis is on maintaining or improving the physical or emotional health of the participants. Sections include goals and objectives of horticultural therapy, suggested year-round programming, indoor and outdoor gardening, nature crafts, and resource materials. These are good books to assist you in facilitating horticultural therapy programs for these populations.

Moore, Bibby, HTR. GROWING WITH GARDENING: "A Twelve Month Guide for Therapy, Recreation and Education." Paper $14.95 U.S.
The University of North Carolina Press 1989
PO Box 2288
Chapel Hill, NC 27515-2288
USA

This book offers the therapist complete, year-round programming. It is particularly great for persons starting programs, providing excellent program content. Sections are broken down into daily activities as well as step-by-step instructions on projects and plant care. There is also an excellent resources list. This book is a must to augment your program.

Morgan, Betty. GROWING TOGETHER: Activities to use in your Horticulture and Horticultural Therapy Programs for Children. Paper: $14.95 U.S.
Pittsburgh Civic Garden Center
1059 Shady Avenue
Pittsburgh, PA 15232
USA

This 310-page book offers the novice gardener the basic skills and activities necessary in horticulture to help conduct HT programs with children and adolescents or those individuals with special needs. The book contains a "recipe-style" of step-by-step instruction for projects. There are sections on plants, basic care, and a reference section for further resource material. This book can assist you in some basic crafts, is easy to read and offers a very straight forward approaches to using exciting mediums with this population.

The "plant expert" books by Dr. D.G. Hessayon, with titles such as: THE BEDDING PLANT EXPERT; THE FLOWER EXPERT; THE TREE & SHRUB EXPERT; have proved invaluable in my work. There are six titles in all, and I strongly recommend them as an easily accessed, up-to-date, well-documented source of information on all aspects of horticulture. (See *Bibliography* ).

HORTICULTURAL THERAPY. Video Course from The Department of Horticulture, College of Agriculture, Kansas State University. Cost: $110 (US)-$45 (US) video tape deposit.
Dr. B. Lockhart
Academic Outreach, Division of Continuing Education
311 Umberger Hall
Kansas State University
Manhattan, Kansas 66506
USA

Kansas State University offers students a video tape correspondence course to provide them with credits towards an undergraduate or graduate credit in horticultural therapy. There are fourteen forty-minute video lectures that provide a variety of subjects pertinent to horticultural therapy.

THE GROWING CONNECTION IN THERAPY. A videotape from the University of Georgia, written material by Chicago Horticultural Society.

Personal Adult Learning Services
Georgia Centre for Continuing Education
University of Georgia
Athens, GA 30602
USA

Program includes a 30-minute videotape and four instructional packages: Horticultural Therapy for the Physically Disabled; for Older Adults, for the Developmentally Disabled; and for Individuals with Mental Illness. Cost: Individual $75 (U.S.)—Complete $250 (U.S.)

## *Suppliers*

Jack Van Klavern
P.O. Box 910
1894 Seventh Street
St. Catharines, Ontario L2R 6Z4
Canada
(905) 641-5599

I have done business with this company for over 20 years. They have knowledgeable staff who can assist you in purchasing the right crops to grow in your environment. This company has large display posters of plants, with well-written information on the culture of a variety of crops. Items that I have found very valuable from this company are "Rocket Packs," an item that is ideal for propagating plants. It consists of a styrofoam container three times the length and thickness of an egg carton and has a series of planting holes. The 26-hole container is excellent for starting cuttings or seeds. Rocket Packs are ideal, as they are lightweight, stable and allow people with visual or perceptual problems to easily and successfully fill and plant them.

Growing Media: Perlite, vermiculite and soilless mediums can be purchased from this company in bulk. I use their grow mix for everything I plant, adding nutrients or other amendments where necessary. This product is light, economical, and nonpoisonous if ingested.

Annuals: Jack Van Klavern sells seed by weight and they are packaged in paper and foil to ensure maximum protection and germination. Annual plants are available in large plastic flats for transplanting into containers for box plants. Small seedlings make transplanting easier for clients who have visual and perceptual deficits. Plants are easily removed from these containers.

The company also supplies Holland bulbs, such as tulips, daffodils, hyacinths and amaryllis.

Plant Products
314 Orenda Road
Brampton, Ontario L6T 1G1
Canada
(905) 793-7000

This company sells a wide variety of products that are used for, or in conjunction with, growing plants. They have a number of items that are excellent for the small solarium or in greenhouse operations.

Plant Products also has a number of chemical products, such as plant growth regulators, disease and pest control as well as natural biological controls, such as insects, i.e., white fly parasites, lady bugs, and predatory mites. They supply Safer's insecticidal soap, a low toxicity insecticide for the control of a variety of insects; safety equipment, such as protective clothing, gloves and industrial masks are available for use when using chemicals; water soluble fertilizers (sold in 15 kilo bags, approximately 33.33 pounds, in a variety of formulations for a variety of crops).

For the greenhouse, they supply Liquid Shade, a product sprayed onto the outside of the glass to control the amount of transmitted light, through greenhouse or solarium windows. This spray protects plants from the burning, destructive rays of the sun.

One item that I would not be without is a product called HOZON. This is a brass siphon mixer that accurately applies fertilizers, pesticides and other water soluble chemicals for use in the greenhouse, lawn and garden. It attaches to the faucet where it automatically siphons up the water and chemicals and expels them through a hose.

White Rose Nurseries

There are White Rose outlets located in most cities and towns across Canada. This company supplies a great number of items from nursery stock and gardening supplies to a plethora of craft items. They have great selection of items to offset horticulturally-related crafts. Watch for their flyers and always plan craft purchases after the seasonal event to get the best buy. This company supports the special events of non-profit organizations that use their products (in making or growing merchandise to be sold to raise money for worthwhile causes).

Richters
Goodwood, Ontario LOC 1A0
Canada
(905) 640-6641

Richters supplies Canada and the United States with an excellent supply of seeds, herb plants, alpine flowers, and a variety of products. They have a full range of supplies for making potpourri, i.e., oils, fixatives and spices. They are also a good resource for posters, books and magazines.

## Mail Orders

The following mail-order companies offer a wide range of quality vegetable and flower seeds:

Stokes
39 James Street
St. Catharines, Ontario L2R 6R6
Canada
(905) 688-4300

Dominion Seed House
P.O. Box 10
Georgetown, Ontario L7G 4A2
Canada
(416) 564-7333

A.E. McKenzie Seeds
Brandon, Manitoba R7A 4A4
Canada
(204) 727-0766

These companies supply to Canada and the United States. Their products consist of a variety of good quality florist supplies, e.g. drieds, birds, ribbons, wreaths, baskets, etc.

Sheldrick's
9206 Dickenson Road
Mount Hope, Ontario L0R 1W0
Canada
(416) 679-4169

Sproule Enterprises
1300 Kamato Road
Mississauga, Ontario L4W 2N2
Canada

For biological control insects contact:

Better Yield Insects
R.R. #3,
Belle River, Ontario N0R 1A0
Canada
(519) 727-6108

This company supplies quality light units adapted for beds and wheelchairs:

Floralight
6-620 Supertest Road
North York, Ontario M3J 2M5
Canada
(416) 665 4000
Fax (416) 665-4003
1-800- 665-4000

For the flower gatherer, contact:

The Added Touch
132 Trafalgar Road
Oakville, Ontario L6J 9Z9
Canada
1-800-268-5060

For more information on Bill 79, or poison control write:

Ministry of Labour
400 University Avenue
Toronto, Ontario M7A 1T7
Canada

Canadian Centre for Occupational Health and Safety
250 Main Street East
Hamilton, Ontario L8N 1H6
Canada

Poison Control Centre
c/o Children's Hospital of Eastern Ontario
401 Smythe Road
Ottawa, Ontario K1H 8L1
Canada
(613) 521-4040

For the USA contact:

OSHA – Occupational Safety and Health Administration, Washington, D.C.

U.S. Poison Control – Look in the telephone directory under the County Government section

# Bibliography

American Psychiatric Association. *Diagnostic and Statistical Manual of Mental Disorders*, (3rd ed., rev.). D.C.: Washington, 1987.

Burlingame, Allice W. *Hoe for Health.* Michigan: Birmingham, Alice W. Burlingame, 3891 Oakhills Drive, 1974.

Daubert, J.R. and Rothert, E.A. *Horticultural Therapy for Senior Centers Nursing Homes Retirement Living.* Illinois: Glencoe, Chicago Horticultural Society, 1981.

Gletiman, Henry. *Psychology.* W.W. Norton & Company, lnc., New York, 1981.

Hessayon, D.G. *The Bedding Plant Expert.* Publications Britannica House, England: Waltham Cross, Herts, 1993.

Hessayon, D.G. *The House Plant Expert.* Publications Britannica House, England: Waltham Cross, Herts, 1992.

Hcssayon, D.G. *The Indoor Plant Spotter.* Publications Britannica, England: Waltham Cross, Herts, 1985.

Hessayon,. D.G. *The Tree and Shrub Expert.* Publications Britannica, England: Waltham Cross, Herts, 1991.

Hessayon,. D.G. *The Vegetable Expert.* Publications Britannica, England: Waltham Cross, Herts, 1990.

Hewson, Mitchell. Horticultural Therapy. *TLC for Plants.* 1990-1993.

Homewood Alcohol and Drug Assessment Literature. Homewood Health Centre Guelph, Ontario, 1993.

Mishel, Nerlove Harriet and Mischel, Walter. *Essentials of Psychology.* Random House, Inc., NewYork, 1977.

Morgan, M.H. and Morgan, H.G. *Aids to Psychiatry.* (3rd ed.). Churchill Livingstone, Inc., New York, 1989.

Natvig, Deborah. *The Role of the Interdisciplinary Team in Using Psychotropic Drugs.* Journal of Psychosocial Nursing 29(10):3-8, 1991.

*Outdoor Plants Harmful or Poisonous to Humans.* Print media Branch, Alberta Agriculture, 7000 113 Street, Edmonton, Alberta, Canada T6H 5T6.

*Poisonous Plants of the U.S. and Canada.* Prentice Hall, Inc., New Jersey: Englewood Cliffs.

Reader's Digest Association. *Magic and Medicine of Plants.* Canada. 1986.

Stone, Evelyn M. *American Psychiatric Glossary.* American Psychiatric Press, Inc. D.C.: Washington. 1988.

Toseland, Ronald W., Palmer-Ganeles, Joan, Chapman, Dennis. *Teamwork in Psychiatric Settings.* Social Work 31 (1):46-52, 1986.

Wright, Barbara Ayn. *Behavior Diagnoses by a Multidisciplinary Team.* Geriatric Nursing 14(1):30-35, 1993.

Wrightsman, Lawrence S., et al. Psychology. *A Scientific Study of Human Behaviour.* Brooks/Cole Publishing Company, California: Monterey. 1979.

# Index

## C

Cacti 50, 52, 122
  *Aporocatuac flagelliformis* (Rat's Tail Cactus) 122
  *Chamascereus silvestrii* (Peanut Cactus) 122
  *Cereus peruvianus monstrosus* (Rock Cactus) 122
  *Echinofossulocactus zacatecasensis* (Brain Cactus) 122
  *Echinocactus* (Barrel Cactus) 122
  *Gymnocalycium mihanovichii var. friedrichii*
    (Red Capped Cactus) 122
  *Lovivia aurea* (Golden Lily Cactus) 122
Calamondin Orange (Dwarf Orange) 49
Calligraphy 132
*Calluna* (Heather) 110
Canada-Wide Volunteer Ontario 138
Canadian Centre for Occupational Health and Safety 144
Canadian Council on Health Facilities Accreditation
  Standards (CCHFA) 25
Canadian Horticultural Therapy Association CHTA 135
Carbamazepine 37
Carnation (*Dianthus*) 118
Castor Bean (*Ricinus*) 76
Cattails 119
Cedar, Young's red 101
  common 101
*Celosia* (*C. plumosa*) 73
*Cereus,* Night Blooming Cactus 29
*Chaenomeles* (Flowering Quince) 106, 107
Chemical Dependancy 33
Cherry (*Prunus*) 73, 106, 107
Chicago Horticultural Society 139
Chinese Evergreen (*Aglaonema*) 50, 78
Chinese Lantern (*Physalis*) 71, 118
Chinese Witch Hazel (*Hamamelis*) 106
Chives (*Allium schoenoprasum*) 61, 79, 125
*Chlorophytum comosum* (Spider Plant) 55, 79, 97, 122
Clothing, protective 38, 142
Clozapine 38
*Cineraria* (Dusty Miller) 72
Cinquefoil (*Potentilla*) 74, 110
*Cissus* sp. 50, 79, 101
  *C. antarctica* (Kangaroo Vine) 50
  *C rhombifolia* (Grape Ivy) 79, 101
*Citrus* (Orange Tree) 122
*Cladonia* (Reindeer Moss) 100
*Codiaeum* (Croton) 76, 122
*Coleus* 50, 79, 108
Combination Plantings (P) 122
Coneflower, Purple (*Echinacea*) 72, 95, 118
Cones, pinecone, hemlock, spruce 112, 119
Containers 52
  aquarium 52, 102
  basket 52, 122

clay 52, 104, 122
demijohn 52, 102
fish bowl 52, 107
plastic 52
pickle jar 52, 102, 106, 129
porcelain 52
rose bowl 52, 102
fruit juice bottle, small 107, 125
*Convallaria* (Lily-of-the-Valley) 76
*Cordyline* (Ti Plant) 122
Corn Plant (*Dracaena*) 50, 55, 78
*Cornus* (Dogwood) 73
*Cornus stolonifera* (Dogwood) 106
Corks 125
*Crassula argentea* (Jade Plant) 34, 50, 79, 123
*Crassula lycopodiodes* (Rat Tail Plant) 123
*Crassula perforata* (String of Buttons) 123
*Crassula rochea var. falcata* (Propeller Plant) 123
Creeping Charlie (*Pilea nummularia folia*) 127
Creeping Jenny (*Pilea depressa*) 101
Crocus 96
Croton (*Codiaeum*) 76, 122
*Cryptanthus* (Earth Star) 102
Cuttings, leaf 53, 54, 108
  stem 54, 108
Cyclic anti-depressants 38

## D

Daffodils 88, 96, 104
*Davallia camaroesmos* (Rabbit's Foot Fern) 100
December 97
*Delphinium* 76, 110, 118, 129
Dementia 30
Depressive illness/affective disorders 29
*Deutzia* 110
*Dianthus* (Pinks) 71
Diazinon 44, 46, 47
*Digitalis* (Foxglove) 76
*Dieffenbachia* (Dumb Cane) 55, 75
Disabled Independent Gardeners Association (DIGA) 136
Division 56
Dock 119
Dogwood, Flowering (*Cornus*) 73
Dogwood (*Cornus stolonifera*) 106
Dominion Seed House 149
*Dracaena* (Corn Plant) 50, 55, 78
Drainage material
  gravel 100, 102
  pebbles 15, 52, 102, 104
  clay chips 52, 104
Dried material 129